To Saba Haftbaradaran
a symbol of steadfastness
and resistance

Azam Hadj Heydari

THE PRICE OF
BEING HUMAN

An Iranian, she fled her fundamentalist family to fight the mullahs

Translated by:
carolyne beckingham

THE PRICE OF
BEING HUMAN

BY: AZAM HADJ HEYDARI
Translated by:
carolyne beckingham
Firs Edition: Winter 2013
copyright: Jean Claud Gawsewitch

ISBN: 978-2-9521711-1-3

HOMA Association
for Publication & Communication

انجمـن همـا   برای نشر و ارتباط

14 –16 Rue Saint Hilaire. B.P.70745 St. Ouen L'Aumone
95004 Cergy–Pontoise Cedex, France
www.homa–association.com
Email: info@homa–association.com

FIRST PART

Daughter of a fundamentalist family

My family

I was born in a traditional and religious family, in a poor quarter of south Tehran, in Shoush Square. My father was a fanatic, a blind supporter of the mullahs[1]. He considered them to be the representatives of religion and thought that rejecting them amounted to rejecting Islam.

My father opposed my going to school because, according to him, I was of more use elsewhere. A girl doesn't need to go to school, he thought. That's why, with those antiquated ideas, as soon as I turned 13,

---

1. Among the Shiites, there is a clergy with a hierarchy, of whom the religious men are generally called mullahs. The highest degree of the hierarchy is the grand ayatollah whose pronouncements on religion are imitated.

he set everything in motion to try to marry me off. Obviously, his dearest wish was to see me marry a mullah. But my mother was a learned and clear-sighted woman. She took our side and defended us, my little sister and me, against my father and my brother. With the little money which she earned sewing for her neighbours and the family, she was able to go on sending us to school. Her leitmotif: advising us to go on and on studying, so as not to be dependent and as unhappy as she was.

My older brother Mohammad, who after my father was considered the head of the family, was a supporter of Khomeini. Later on he put himself entirely at the service of the mullahs' regime to become an interrogator and torturer at Evin Prison. Not only was he behind my arrest, but he also personally participated in my torture and in the interrogations I underwent. As my eyes were blindfolded and he was wearing a mask, he thought I couldn't recognise him. Well, from the first moment, I felt his sinister presence through the questions I was asked, as well as that of my cousins also interrogators and torturers at the prison, who were torturing me. In fact, this suspicion became a conviction when, at one point, I managed to pull off my bandage and saw my cousin Aziz. But I shall describe that in more detail later on.

I'm willing to make it understood in what family I was born and brought up. A fanatical and religious family impregnated with the ideology of the mullahs which ascribes no value to women and for whom the latter have been created only to fulfil the desires of men. In the concept, a woman has no identity. Before marriage, she has her father's identity. After marriage, that of her husband. And even after the latter's death, she still has no identity of her own, but is recognised through one of her sons whose name she will bear. A woman has only one rôle: doing the cooking, the washing up, the laundry, everything the man needs, bearing his children and bringing them up. In many households in our neighbourhood, the men didn't call their wives by their first names, but by their son's names, for example "mummy Hassan". Another solution, which I think worse still: they called them simply "woman"! In some families, they even give the wife a masculine name which is usually that of a dead child.

In this kind of family, both love and affection are unknown. In my case, this lack came only from my father and my brothers. But with my mother and my sisters – one older and the other younger than I – we felt love and tenderness for one another, no doubt reinforced by that common sorrow, and we stood together against such a "father" and such "brothers", totally under the spell of the mullahs' ideology.

From my childhood, I remember only a cold and gloomy world. The picture I had of life was summed up by the way we lived and what we saw. I therefore thought that a woman's destiny, because she was a woman, was to be eternally humiliated by men and subject to them. A man who began by calling himself father, then brother, then husband, and as age increased, he became that son one had given birth to and brought up! This sorrowful life was embodied by that of my mother, who was a living example of it.

Revolt against big brother

From my earliest childhood, ever since I began to know, as they say, my left hand from my right, I was in conflict with my brothers and therefore tried to build myself a new life. A life where humanity, love and mutual help would be permissible. Consequently, I tried with all the means that came into my head to resist those creatures who were "brothers" only in name. I remember that when I was in second form at school at the age of thirteen, my eldest brother Mohammad decided to make me go to a religious meeting to which he was going, supposedly for the benefit of my education. But I had understood that the only aim of this kind of teaching was indoctrinating the participants, by forcing them to absorb the conceptions of another age: dedicating themselves to the cult of sadness, beating their chests, flagellating themselves and accepting miserable poverty as a test from the Lord on the way leading to Paradise! Which, in spite of my lack of knowledge and my young age, aroused in me a deep feeling of rejection. The subject of the meeting was patience in the face of miserable poverty. An interesting fact: the woman who called herself the teacher was herself in total contradiction with what she said. For example, she wore an enormous amount of jewellery. It was so screamingly obvious that, in spite of my young age, I said to her in protest:

"Why should I behave as you say, accept this life and tolerate miserable poverty while you are so rich?!"

In my eyes it was perfectly logical. But she answered me that I was an impertinent little thing and sent me out of the room. That suited me perfectly, and I never went back to a meeting of that kind, but by doing so I attracted thunder and lightning from Mohammad who said that I had dishonoured him in the eyes of those to whom he mattered.

After that, Mohammad, in spite of everything, tried several times to make me go to more meetings and religious ceremonies that he was fond of. When I was in the 4th form, he took me to "Sadeghieh", a fundamentalist religious teaching association, where I only stayed a week, as it was so extremely fanatical. A year or two later, my brother pushed me into the claws of the "Hojatieh[2]". I regarded their activities and opinions as vulgar and nothing about them attracted me. And, when I learned that some of their influential elements were rolling in money, I simply decided not to go there again.

That's how Mohammad failed in all his efforts, including that of persuading me to marry one of his friends who shared his opinions. Seeing that during my years at school I had begun to read books that he considered heretical, at home I had become the one who had disobeyed and questioned my big brother's hegemony. From now on I was superfluous and no longer had any rights. To force me to get back in line, not only had he cut off all my financial support, but he had also, through his influence, turned my father against me. So my father considered giving

2. An extremist sect which developed in the Shah's time with the support of the Savak (the political police). The Shah's aim in developing it in religious circles that were naturally opposed to him was to turn the religious young people's potential for protest towards the struggle against the Baha'i, whom the mullahs regarded as heretics. The regime's present president, Mahmous Ahmadinehad, was an active member of Hajatieh.

me any money that could be used for studying and daily life to be sinful. For example, I had to beg my mother, who unfortunately could not help me, several times for the 300 tomans[3] for school expenses. In spite of that, I went on studying. I remember: when the teacher called me to go to the blackboard to answer questions, I said I didn't know the answer and didn't go for fear of showing my badly damaged shoes.

My father and my brother, who felt ferocious hatred for us and didn't spare us the tiniest form of pressure, showed kindness and generosity to those on their side. So my brother consented to pay all the medical expenses for a neighbour's son who suffered from strabismus, and took him to hospital. The latter was devoted to him and shared the mullahs' conceptions. While for me, who was his sister and had the same health problem, he never did or spent anything.

Even if he was now living elsewhere, he had kept his supremacy in his father's house, and as he thought it was his duty to watch over

---

3. 10 rials equal one toman. One euro = 150 tomans.

my little sister Najmeh and me, he had the keys of the house. He always came unexpectedly; we suddenly found ourselves faced with his sarcasm and a prey to his harassment.

My other brother Ali, who was younger than Mohammad, but older than Najmeh and I, lived with us. He too was a supporter of Khomeini. I had even seen him in a group of cosh-wielders who had attacked us in the street. But he didn't really believe in Khomeini. It was only because he was continually under Mohammad's influence and in order to ensure an income for himself that he had chosen his side. But, in practice, he wasn't as virulent as Mohammad.

During the five and a half years that I spent in prison, my father and my two brothers only came to see me once, and that was to warn me that I must give in. Otherwise, it would mean the death penalty. They thought I would yield, because I was in the hands of the torturers. As soon as they arrived behind the window of the visitors' room, they questioned my convictions and my goals, told me that I was solely responsible for what was happening to me and that I must repent because that road could lead only to my death.

Hearing them, I thought that not answering them would be a sign of weakness and that it would encourage them. I told myself that one only died once. I hadn't come in order to stay alive, so it was better to die with my convictions intact rather than in a state of humiliation. I broke silence to defend my ideas and my organisation[4], and told them everything that was on my mind.

That time, they kept quiet, and left without even turning back. After that, they never came again, saying that I was a "*Monafegh*[5]" and condemned to death.

On the day of that precious visit, with the aim of breaking me down, they had brought me some worn-out clothes, coming from I don't know where. I really needed them, but I preferred to throw them all away.

Fortunately, in the group of the supporters

---

4. I belonged to the People's Mojahedin of Iran organisation, a progressive Muslim movement which has become the main opposition to Khomeini's regime.

5. *Monafegh*, literally "hypocrite", a pejorative term that the mullahs' regime uses to designate the People's Mojahedin of Iran.

of the Mojahedin, love, friendship and kindness reigned. For example, throughout the time of my punishment when I had no visits, everyone who received some clothes put the best aside for me, and I never knew from whom they came.

The misogyny at the heart of the cruelty of Khomeini's supporters

As I have said, my father and my brother were fierce supporters of Khomeini's ideology. I can never explain to what extent this ideology empties people of their affection for their families, and gives them a heart of stone. Whole pages on the subject wouldn't suffice. My father, for example, forbade himself to show any sign of interest and tenderness or love towards us. He thought that kissing a child made it insolent. As far back as I can remember, he never kissed my sister or me once. I never understood why. I didn't understand either why my father and my brothers were so cruel, pitiless and devoid of affection not only towards my sisters and me, but also towards my mother who worked so hard for them. At the time, I didn't know that misogyny was at the heart of the mullahs' barbarous and retrograde conception and that it fed that way of behaving.

My mother's speedy death at the age of 56 was caused by that lack of affection and that misogyny. For several days, my mother hadn't been feeling well and complained of chest pains. But we knew that so long as her illness didn't make her fall down, there would be no question of calling the doctor. It didn't enter our heads, either hers or ours, to go and consult the doctor ourselves. Until the day when she fainted in the yard of our house. I flew to help her and tried to lead her inside, but as I hadn't the strength, I ran to tell my brother that our mother was ill and that she was lying on the ground in the yard. He answered coldly that she must have eaten something bad and that it wasn't serious. My father, who was concerned about going to Paradise, was reading the Qur'an and didn't budge an inch. When I saw that they weren't reacting and that my mother's life was of no importance in their eyes, I quickly went to ask our neighbour for help. Together with my big sister, all three of us led her, but far too late, to the hospital near the house. Mummy had had a coronary. She should have been transferred to a specialist hospital. We didn't have the means to do it, and we had to leave her in that hospital which had no cardiology unit. After five days, this woman who had suffered so much died of a fresh attack, while my brother had ample means to put her in a cardiology unit and save her.

After my mother's death, my sister and I lost our only support and the burden of life grew much heavier. The only person who, during that period, replaced our mother to some extent was my big sister Mahine, eleven years my senior. Najmeh and I grew closer together, and as I was being paid a salary, I took care of her. She then went with me to nearly all my activities. Najmeh was a very intelligent and very dynamic girl. She began, when the uprising against the Shah's dictatorship developed, to take part alone in political activities. Thanks to the revolution and the movement which was agitating society, a channel opened in our dark and sad life. A channel in which to breathe the fresh air of freedom, a channel bringing the light of hope for the liberation of women.

The stolen revolution

The theft of the leadership of the anti-monarchist revolution that Khomeini committed has already caused a lot of ink to flow. But I who come from a fanatically religious family, believing in Khomeini as hard as iron, I can swear that neither my father nor my brothers, who supported the mullahs when they achieved power, were ever revolutionaries. Not only did they not go to dangerous places, but they prevented the young people in the family from participating. The agitation at the time of the revolution was essentially young people's doing. They were the ones at the heart of the action, in the front line, and the ones who were getting killed. They too were the ones who, after the revolution, were slaughtered in prison, this time not by the Shah but by Khomeini's executioners. Everyone remembers 8 September 1978, Black Friday, and the bloodbath in Tehran. I remember that neither my father nor my brothers went there and that they would not give us, the younger ones, permission to leave the house. For the Shah's regime had decreed a curfew and everyone knew that this day wouldn't be like the rest.

On 8 September 1978, I, who couldn't bear to stay at home, was crying and asking my father and my brothers to let me go out and join the people. But they wouldn't let me go, telling me it was too dangerous and that I would be killed. At the time, when I was 20 years old and had my baccalaureate, I didn't dare go out or do anything without their permission, and I was afraid of them. But when I learned about the mass killing of men, defenceless women and the children in their arms, and when I learned that there were demonstrators among my own circle, I regretted not having gone and I asked myself why I had asked my father's and brothers' permission.

That day, something changed in

me. The very next day, I took part in the demonstrations without their permission. Certainly, I still did it in secret: I left and came back before they came home. Taking part in the demonstrations, in contact with men and women in search of liberty and willing to pay the price for it, little by little I grew braver. I saw in that revolution and its slogans all my hopes as an oppressed and humiliated young woman, and thought I had found what I sought in the insurrection and the serried ranks of the processions. For at that time I was imprisoned in my home, not only physically but also mentally. My world consisted of my home and the school nearby. Even during the journey from home to school, I didn't raise my head to look at my surroundings because I had heard it said, and it had become a value anchored in my deepest being, that a well-brought-up young girl must never raise her head. I was afraid that, if my father or my brothers saw me in the street with my head up, I could never go to school again. I have already said it: my father seriously believed that school was bad for girls. My little sister and I, who had obtained permission to go there only through my mother's support, dreaded that this fragile privilege, acquired with difficulty by means of tears and supplications and my mother's support at the beginning of each school year, would go up in smoke if there was any mistake.

That's how I was able to get my baccalaureate. The only job that my family and social situation would allow me to take was that of a teacher. Teaching, especially at the girls' school, where there was no contact with men, was acceptable to my father. Besides, for a poor family like ours, additional income was welcome, and my father obviously couldn't oppose it. I adored my job; I loved children and wanted to help them, especially the most disadvantaged. During that short period when I worked, the terrifying face of poverty and its consequences became more familiar to me. I, who thought I knew about poverty because of my family's living conditions, began to understand that there was a far deeper and more tragic poverty that affected millions of people, and above all women and little girls.

The school where I taught was an elementary school in one of the poorest and remotest quarters in the south of the capital. The children at that school went to bed with their bellies empty and arrived in the morning with hunger clawing at them. They had worn-out shoes and clothes that completely failed to protect them from the cold. The little girls in my class sometimes slid under the tables and began to cry with heavy sobs. They didn't dare say they were hungry. I, who had come to teach them, saw the monster of poverty and hunger. I asked myself how I could teach anything to a starving child, white as a sheet, or one who was weeping with cold, a child who watched her parents quarrelling every day over their daily bread, and witnessed the blows her father dealt to her mother. Sometimes I helped them out of my modest means, or brought them something to eat, but there were many of them and all that couldn't be solved in a day. Faced with that want, I felt powerless. I reflected for hours on what I could do in the face of that dramatic situation that the plague of want had created for those little girls, so sweet and so adorable. In vain.

SECOND PART

Another world

A meeting with the People's Mojahedin

Because of the restraints from which I suffered in my childhood and throughout my youth, at the time of the revolution, aged 20, I never went far from the house for fear of being lost in the town. During the uprising, when I went out, my only concern was to know how I was going to come back. I must not lose my way. Participating in the anti-royalist demonstrations enabled me to discover a new word. An interesting, varied new world with fascinating and friendly people, who taught me many things, a world which captivated me more every day.

One day, in a demonstration, I met a

girl who was quite unlike any of the women I had known up till then. She seemed bold, independent and confident. Fascinated by her personality, I followed her. I asked her to lead me wherever she went. Tahereh, as she was called, was astonished at first.

"Well everyone's going there, you go there too," she said to me.

I begged her:

"No! I want to come with you, I don't know the way."

In her face, courage and combativeness mingled with goodness and kindness, which hitherto I had never seen in anyone, least of all a woman. She didn't laugh at my ignorance but, rather, encouraged me to learn and experiment. To be at her side was an opportunity for me and I felt strong. I had discovered in her a form of support and did everything not to lose her. Once, I asked her insistently:

"So you haven't told me where you're going tomorrow. I want to come with you too."

She accepted with a smile, and next day

and on the following days I went with her.

Tahereh opened up a new chapter in my life. A new universe, totally different from what I knew: the world of militarism. For Tahereh was a supporter of the People's Mojahedin of Iran[1].

Towards the end of the uprising, when I came back from demonstrations or remained at school to work there and came home later than expected, my father asked my big sister, grumbling:

"Why's Azam still out at this hour of the night?"

And he shouted at her, as throughout his

---

1. The People's Mojahedin were founded in 1965 by intellectuals who supported the great democratic leader, Mohammad Mossadegh, who nationalised Iranian oil. Recommending a tolerant and democratic form of Islam, they opposed the dictatorship of the Shah who executed its founders and many of its members. After the revolution, they found a great response among Iranian youth, and became the first political force to opposed the dictatorship of the mullahs. The People's Mojahedin refused to endorse the theocratic Constitution and the principle of a supreme leader as guardian of the people. This refusal earned them a very harsh repression lasting until today. Over 120,000 of their members and supporters were executed by this regime. On 20 June 1981, Khomeini ordered the slaughter of a large peaceful demonstration of 500,000 supporters of the PMOI at Tehran, suppressing all possibility of legal opposition. The People's Mojahedin then formed a Resistance. The director of the PMOI who made history, Massoud Rajavi, founded in July 1981 at Tehran the coalition of the National Council of the Iranian Resistance which recommended a secular and pluralist republic, with equality of women and men and respect for human rights.

life he had shouted at my mother who was no longer in this world.

At the time, my father was already reproaching me for my work outside the home, my fighting and the fact that I wanted to choose my life freely. But, because of the demonstrations, of my meeting with Tahereh and everything I had learned from her, I wasn't what I had been. I was the new Azam. I had courage now, and I had decided to fight for my freedom, and to fight against my father, my brothers and their retrograde and ossified convictions. But I hadn't begun total opposition. I still dreaded the archaic traditions against which I wanted to rise. Confronting, in the street, the Shah's armed soldiers who sometimes opened fire on the crowd and caused deaths, needed much less courage than fighting my father, the family traditions and the world I belonged to. That possibly arose from the fact that in the street I wasn't alone, I was surrounded by thousands of people who offered help and support in case of need. But at home, faced with the appalling force which emanated from my father and my brothers, my sister and I felt alone and defenceless.

During the last days, I put on a black chador for going out, but once outside and far away from my street, I took it off and put it in a bag so as to be able to move freely and run. Now, for my family, the headscarf wasn't regarded as a hijab sufficient to preserve a woman's modesty, and I was constantly afraid of what could happen if they saw me in the street without a chador. I told myself that if it were to happen, I should die of fright. Every time I came home, two or three streets before ours, I went into a corner to put my chador back on, taking care that nobody should see me committing that mortal sin, and report it. Those moments of fear and anguish weren't, however, without a certain pleasure: the feeling of seeing new pathways open and being able to overcome obstacles. A feeling of being alive.

First revolt

One day, with a friend, we decided to go, together with her brother who was driving a car full of tracts and books, to demonstrate at the Behecht Zahra cemetery at the tomb of the martyrs of the revolution. To go out without my father noticing, I had to play hide and seek with him. Once outside, we left for the cemetery. Leaving the house had been, for me, like climbing a mountain. We shouted slogans against the Shah and his regime with joy and energy, and we hurried to pass the police station. But after a few metres, at a turning, policemen who barred the way ordered us to turn round. They led us to the police station before making us get out of the car. And there, in front of the door, they started to hit us with the butts of their guns. At that precise moment, I felt strong in front of the policemen who were hitting us, because I was engaged in fighting and taking part myself in the popular uprising. But on the other hand I was trembling all over because I was terrified at the idea that they might detain us overnight and that I couldn't go home. I didn't know what I should say to my father. All that disturbed me. Because my father said that a girl who studies is useless, it was easy to imagine what he would say about a girl who got herself arrested. Seized with devouring anguish, I asked my friend what we should do if they didn't free us when evening fell.

"Don't worry," she answered, "we'll see."

"But what shall I say to my father?"

"Listen, this really isn't the moment! First we'll see what happens, then we'll deal with that too. Azam, please, don't think about it, right?"

Her firmness and confidence gave me back my strength and I was happy to have someone on whom I could count in case of trouble. As she had understood, she soothed me with her words and told me not to worry, that nothing would happen and she would answer my father.

Not only did the police not free us that evening, but they kept us in prison for three days.

At the end of three days, when they freed us, I had the feeling that I had solved a big problem by going out without my father's permission. In spite of everything, once outside, I couldn't help saying:

"I'm dead of fright! How can I go back home now? What shall I tell my father and my brother?"

My friend suggested coming with me. But I told myself: *why must I be escorted like a child? Go on! Take courage, go by yourself and answer your father and your brother!* So It old her that I had changed my mind, that she could go, that I should cope and that I wanted to speak to them alone. She tried for a long time to convince me to let her come and calm my father, but I had decided: I must succeed! All the same I came home trembling. That was when I saw my father and my brother, tense-faced; they stood up suddenly, certainly in order to hit me. I tried to face them. I told myself continually: *You can do it! Don't be afraid! Wasn't it you who said that you wanted to fight against that? What's done is done, go to it! Let them see you're not the same Azam! As they say, you only die once. And that's what I did.*

I was afraid but I didn't show it, I went up and said hello. I waited to see what they would say. When they had covered me with insults and dragged me in the mud, and came towards me to hit me, I prepared myself to answer. But when they asked me where I was, I was afraid and said that I was with a friend. My father howled.

"You'll pay dearly for it! A girl doesn't stay out at night, who gave you permission?!"

I regretted not having told the truth. Then I took the plunge and answered in a firm voice, like a stranger:

"I was at the police station! Yes, I was in prison, at the police station! You did say it was war? Well, I'm one of the people too and I want to fight!"

My father, who wasn't expecting that answer, remained dumbstruck for a few moments. As they had come up to me, they slapped me and rained punches and kicks on me. Having nothing left to lose, I cried out in a strong voice, sure of myself:

"Why are you hitting me? I have rights too! How can you be content to watch people dying without taking action?"

My words must have had an effect as

they stopped hitting me father than I would have believed.

My father sat down fulminating:

"It's all my fault for letting you study and work, from the first day onwards. A girl who studies and leaves the house is no longer any use."

The beginning of a long fight

That is how I made my way out of the house. With Tahereh and the friends I had made on demonstrations, I participated in almost all the popular protests. After Tahereh, I came to know more and more militant girls and women of the People's Mojahedin, who taught me a great deal. I had the impression that I was no longer alone on that road; I felt I had a lot of support. Those who surrounded me understood me and I could ask them for help. They didn't humiliate me because I was a woman, I had value in their eyes and they gave me the right to choose.

I was no longer afraid of my father or my brother. Later on, even in the terrible moments I lived through, above all with that "non-brother" torturer, I told myself that we'd see who would end up winning! As for me, I didn't have the shadow of a bout: I was going to win! Because I was the one who had chosen. I had tasted the bitterness of that imprisoned life for every moment of twenty long years, and I knew that I would never go back to that existence, that prison, that black closed world, with its limited horizon, in a constant state of humiliation, in a word to life in a tomb!

I had emerged victorious from my first battle for independence from my father and my brothers, but it was only the start of a long fight. Because until the revolution, there were still some points on which I agreed with them. At first, one might have believed that by going to demonstrate, I was in favour of a revolution under Khomeini's direction. But in the next stages of the fight, which were to prove more violent and bloodier, the way and the ideas that I had chosen, namely the People's Mojahedin and their ideas, were opposed to Khomeini and his ideology. That was when I entered into total war, especially against my brother.

Day by day I was more attracted to the Mojahedin. Apart from the times when I was teaching at the school near my home, I devoted the rest of my time to the organisation. I stayed out late some evenings, I spent most of my time in the street demonstrating, selling newspapers and books or taking part in the courses that the organisation ran for its militant members. I devoured this new life with avidity, minute by minute. I was like someone on the brink of suffocation who suddenly found some air. I felt myself existing. I was of use for something and that made me happy.

Certainly, at home, there were still conflicts and quarrels with my father and brother. On the pretext that a girl shouldn't stay outside and speak to strangers, they threatened to settle my hash.

"If we see you in the street too like the girls in the "movement", talking politics and selling newspapers, you've had it."

In my heart, I laughed in their faces: did they think that with those threats, they could stop me freeing myself and leading the life I had chosen? But fear gripped me.

One day when I had gone to sell the *Mojahed*[2] paper in Khorassan Square, in our quarter, I was arrested. It is one of the most traditional quarters in Theran, and I think that was where one found the greatest number of agents of the Committees, of the Bassij[3] militia, of Khomeini's phalangists and of cosh-wielders. That day, with two of my friends, Kobra and Zahra Ebrahimian, we had begun to sell the newspaper. As usual, we were auctioning the copies. Suddenly we saw twenty or thirty of Khomeini's Pasdaran[4] and Hezbollahis[5]. They threw themselves at us and hit us savagely. At the same time they tried to snatch the newspapers from us and tear them up. The Pasdaran tore us to pieces, but they didn't manage to take the

2. Organ of the PMOI (People's Mojahedin Organisation of Iran).

3. The Committees are a kind of police station of the Bassij militia.

4. The Body of Revolutionary Guards or "Pasdaran" designates the ideological army founded by Khomeini in order dominate the regular army inherited from the old regime and lead the repression of the opposition. (See Mehdi Abrichamchi's very detailed work, *The Revolutionary Guards*, published by Jean Picollec.)

5. The Hezbollahis are groups of gangsters paid by the regime. Often they are Pasdaran in civilian clothes.)

newspapers, because we protected them by forming a rampart of our own bodies, as if our lives depended on it. I even had some left in my hand when I was arrested.

I was taken to the Committee on Khorassan Square. I had chosen to fight but I was still very frightened of situations like these, of finding myself in the quarter's Committee, which my father and my brothers regarded as a stain on the family honour. When I entered the Committee, the cosh-wielders and Hezbollahis looked at one another, amazed. They said: "Ah! It's so and so's daughter, so and so's sister," because our family had been living in the quarter of twenty years and everyone knew us. Then they started to frighten me by threatening to call my father and my brothers.

At first I was terrified: at home we were three women faced with three men. In front of the men of the family, I felt weak. I did everything to stop them knowing about my activities, but I had entered into a battle, and henceforward, whether I wanted it or not, my fighting set me up against them. To speak the truth, there was also a conflict inside me. Khomeini or the Mojahedin? The choice of one or the other corresponded to a totally different way of life. If I chose Khomeini, I was going to a mournful life between the four walls of a house, and I, a teacher, had to say goodbye to my work. On the whole it would be a life without problems. I should be rid of the conflicts at home and the conflicts outside with the Pasdaran and Khomeini's supporters, of the same type as my father and my brothers. But if I chose the Mojahedin, I was entering into a dangerous and implacable fight. A fight for freedom which demanded an iron will, but which also had all its flavour. At that moment, I could not imagine for a second what would happen to me later. But I knew more or less that it would be an arduous and dangerous path, and more than once I asked myself if I could go on to the end. All the same, in the depths of my being, I was very happy. The incidents and the problems that occurred were certainly painful, but every time I had the feeling of having rounded a cape and feeling enlarged and alive as a result.

Once, our team which was selling *Mojahed* papers in Abmangal Street in Tehran, one of the HQs of the Pasdaran and of those savages in the Committee, was attacked by some Hezbollahis and Pasdaran. Among them, I recognised Askar Oladi[6] who, with his terrifying eyes, was looking us up and down. I think he recognised me. I was afraid for a moment, always the same fear of my father, my brothers and the family. At the same moment, my eyes fell on Azar, a girl in the team, who was fighting like a lioness against the Pasdaran and the regime's agents. She had risen up in front of them to protect us. Her daring and firmness gave me courage, and I too decided to be like her, and that was the moment when I felt that I was capable of no longer fearing those jackals.

They took us to the Committee of Abmangal and until the evening they hit us to much that Azar's face and body were covered with bruises. The other two young women and I were in no better state. It was

---

6. Askar Oladi is one of the leaders of the fundamentalist tendency, a member of the State Council of Judgment, to whom I am distantly related.

on that occasion that I discovered for the first time the violence of the hatred and the animal ferocity of Khomeini's supporters towards the Mojahedin. I understood that, when the moment came, they wouldn't forbear to commit any crime against us and they wouldn't for one moment hesitate to kill us. Now that was happening at a time when the organisation's activities were not yet forbidden. The newspaper was still allowed to be published. That was precisely what we had denounced: we were doing nothing illegal! That's why they freed us at the end of the afternoon.

Once outside, I was afraid in spite of everything to go home with my wounded face, covered with bruises. I didn't know what to say to my father and my brothers! But while doing this, I asked myself why I should be frightened. It was for them to tell me if that was the Islam they spoke of. Was that their Muslim dignity? Taking innocent, defenceless girls to the Committee where enormous, savage men threw themselves on them to hit them pitilessly? Because, after all, what was our crime?

Another time, in Taleghani Street, I was walking with Zohreh Tabrizi[7], my fellow team member, right in the middle of the cars which were waiting at a red light. We were auctioning copies of the *Mojahed* newspaper, when suddenly I found myself face to face with my older brother who was looking very nervously at me from inside a car. I had asked myself several times what would happen on the day when my brother saw me fighting for the Mojahedin. What would he do? And how would I react? It had happened at the moment when I least expected it. I lost all my powers and stopped. Zohreh, who was a little in front of me, seeing me fall suddenly silent, asked me what was happening. I showed her the car and told her that it was my brother. Zohreh, who knew the story of my dealings with my brother and my family, answered me:

"Come on, pay no attention. If he dares, all he needs to do is get out of the car. As to us, the people are with us!"

---

7. She was executed in 1981.

Zohreh's words comforted me. I repeated to myself: *She's right, the people are with us, I'm no longer alone here.* I think that he realised it too and preferred to behave as though he hadn't seen me. But I shouted even more loudly: "*Mojahed!* The organ of the People's Mojahedin of Iran!" and went on working in the middle of the cars. That evening, on the way home, I prepared myself for a bloody battle. When I arrived, I deliberately put down the rest of the papers on the television set. My brother said to me:

"Little girl, if I see you once more in the street with those papers, it's the end of you. Do what you like, but not in the street."

In my heart I laughed, feeling victorious: if he had wanted to act and had had the courage, why hadn't he done it today?

I felt strong: his threats no longer frightened me. His presence in my mind had been considerably reduced, like shagreen. It was as if, during this long battle, I was freeing myself every day from chains which shackled my hands and feet. I was standing up, I was gaining independence. This amazing feeling enabled me to deal more easily with problems and dangers, but it also fed my violent revolt against a world dating from an obsolete period, with oppressive and misogynistic practices.

I had reached the point of using everything to fight against that world. For example, coming home late had become a battle. Every day, at home, my delays caused quarrels, but I didn't want to yield an inch of what I considered as a right. Our house, as I have said, was in one of the remote points of the south part of the town. In the evening, I came home late from my work in West Tehran. In my neighbourhood, for a girl, it was almost unthinkable to be still out at a late hour: it was considered a dreadful sin and the men in my family didn't accept my behaviour.

At first, when I came home, I opened the door softly with my key, without making a noise, and I did the housework or had dinner to show that I had been there for a long time. But after a year I said to myself: *why play at hide and seek? It's my right. Why not fight for it?* From that moment on, when I came home, I opened the door normally, I even slammed it, and as the house was small, everyone knew that I had come home. Finally that taboo was broken too. They were obliged to recognise my right.

Happy days of war

In spite of those difficult times, I spent some great moments.

My father was an indefatigable worker and had his good side. In fact, he only lacked knowledge. He thought, for instance, that Khomeini and the mullahs who surrounded him were the only people who knew the truth of Islam. His severity towards me was dictated by his faith, according to him. That's why, one day, I tried to explain to him the way in which the Mojahedin saw Islam. I brought back home a cassette from the philosophy course on the precepts of Islam to which a responsible person in the organisation was letting us listen. When I showed it to him, he refused to listen to it at first. But once the tape began to run, he grew interested in what was being said. His behaviour changed as it went on: first the cassette captured his attention then progressively captivated him, and finally it altogether fascinated him. When it ended, he said to me with astonishment and admiration:

"Yes, they are Muslims, so I don't know what I'm saying, but if I'm a Muslim, then I don't know what they're saying."

He listened to the cassette several times and revealed to me that it was when listening to its contents that he understood the meaning of prayer. From that moment on, he changed his mind about the Mojahedin. He appreciated them and, when my friends came to the house, he received them in a polite and friendly way. He no longer bothered me about my activities and no longer quarrelled with me when I came home late. He had understood that, in my actions with the Mojahedin, he had nothing to fear from a moral point of view.

Another of my great joys at that period when I was supporting the Mojahedin, active night and day, was when I came home late in the evening after a harassing day. My sister Najmeh and her husband Farhad, who had just got married, were there, and Mahine, my big sister, who came to join us. We settled down to tell one another what we had been doing, our experiences, the interesting things we had seen or heard. We also talked about the attacks and assaults of the cosh-wielders, the people's support, and one thing and another. Especially as our activities weren't in the same districts: I was in West Tehran, Najmeh in the south, Farhad in the north, and we worked among different social levels. We argued passionately for hours, we learned from one another and we were wildly happy. My sister Mahine listened to it all with enthusiasm and shared our happiness. As she said later, those days were the happiest of her life, especially as my brothers were no longer living at home and our father was alone. He rested in a room next to us. It exasperated him not to know what we were talking and laughing about until dawn, but he couldn't do anything about it.

Yes, those were truly happy days. But

when Khomeini, whose influence had rooted itself in the minds of my father and people like him for years, appeared on television in 1980 to denounce the Mojahedin openly and call them "hypocrites", his demagogy managed to influence the retrograde religious levels of society, to turn them against the Mojahedin, and to kill all human feelings and family links in them. To the extent that my father then began forbidding me to touch the bread and food he brought, for fear that I should sully them.

Khomeini had understood that if he left the Mojahedin more time, they would cause his social base, founded on ignorance, to melt and disappear. He therefore didn't stop short at any crime to separate the Mojahedin from the Iranian political and social scene. But, finally, it was his inconceivable crimes against their rights and those of the people that rapidly caused him to lose the privileged connection he had woven with the people. In fact, that demagogue, who made the poor and disinherited masses believe that his picture was reflected in the moon, fell into the gutter.

He was rejected by the whole population and made a choice niche for himself among the "worst dictators of the 20th century" in the eyes of the whole international community.

The devaluation of Khomeini's image cost a great deal, however. A price that the Mojahedin and the Iranians in general paid with the flesh and blood of the best among them.

An iron arm between two forces

At the beginning of 1981, the number of attacks by the revolutionary guards and Khomeini's hooligans against the Mojahedin and their supporters grew even greater. Not a day passed without one's being beaten up in the street. And not a day without Mojahedin supporters being killed or wounded, arrested and tortured by Khomeini's cosh-wielders. They punched and kicked us and had a whole panoply of cold steel which bore witness to their intention of killing us.

One day, I was selling the newspaper at the Jomhouri Street crossroads with a friend. She was holding a copy in her hand and, as usual, was auctioning them. On my side, I was responsible for her safety. Suddenly, I saw three well-built and bearded men, who must have been 70 cm taller than I, coming towards us. One of them had his hand in his shirt. I understood that his intentions were bad, and that he wanted to catch hold of something to hit her. I didn't take my eyes off them, and asked myself what I should do. I went behind them. They were a few steps from her when one of them took a nunchaku[8] from his shirt and raised his arm to hit her with all his strength. I don't know how I managed to jump, but I caught the nunchaku in flight from behind and ran away. Jomhouri Street was full of people. I ran as fast as possible, pursued by two of the monsters. I was breathless, exhausted and terrified. Because part of that weak woman's spirit still remained in me, I wished with all my heart that a strong man would come to my help and save me. I didn't know what to do and my headlong flight wasn'e leading anywhere.

---

8. An Asian weapon consisting of two pieces of wood tied together with a chain.

Suddenly, I saw a bridge and a little walkway over the gutter. That was my chance: I threw the nunchaku under it while continuing my flight, but the two monsters soon caught up with me and beat me up. If I was bruised all over, I felt in the depths of my heart that I had won: I had saved my friend, I had taken their weapon, and that was what was driving them mad. Above all they were exasperated that a girl had stood up to them. Little by little, people gathered around us to protest: why were they hitting a poor defenceless girl?

All these events were repeated time and again during my militant activities. Every time, they enabled me to gather strength and assurance. I realised that the people's opinion was changing in parallel, in our favour and against the regime. People saw clearly how the regime's cosh-wielders were behaving to us and hated them for it. Above all, they witnessed our resistance and respected us more, especially the women and girls who supported the Mojahedin, and thus found more courage to oppose the regime's agents. In that immense campaign which extended to the whole of society and to all the towns, we could see how Khomeini fell daily from his pedestal, and how those who loved him at first realised what he was and rallied to the various progressive groups that existed then, the People's Fedayin, the Marxists or the groups that had emerged from the nationalist National Front, or the organisations defending the ethnic minorities such as the Kurds who later responded to the People's Mojahedin's invitation to constitute the coalition of the National Council of Resistance.

From day to day, the savagery and the violence of the Pasdaran and the cosh-wielders towards us increased. When we went out in the morning to sell papers or distribute tracts, we were aware that we had little chance of coming home at night. And it wasn't rare for us to come home with broken limbs or covered in bruises. But thanks to the people's support, our motivation was at its peak. The regime's exasperation was palpable.

Massive arrests

On 31 May 1981, the Pasdaran came to

the school where I taught to arrest me. A colleague notified me. As the window of her classroom looked onto the street, she realised that some odd-looking people were walking round the school. I looked through the pane and I understood that they had come for me. I jumped out of the window and ran from the school at top speed. From that day onwards, I was pursued by the Pasdaran. As I hadn't given the end-of-year examination to the children, I was anxious about their future. I made arrangements with colleagues to organise the exams. In spite of the serious risks that it involved and against my friends' advice, I took the plunge. I no longer wanted to leave the children in a state of uncertainty, so I went back to the school and organised the exam. When the children saw me, they pressed themselves around me. They were pleased to see me. Before leaving them, I explained to them that no doubt I was no longer going to be their teacher, that perhaps we shouldn't see one another again for a long time. The children, very sadly, some with tears I their eyes, thanked me, hoping that I would be their mistress again the next year. It was very hard for me to cut myself off from those little darlings, so sweet and so poor, but I said goodbye to them and went off at top speed, escaping once again from the Pasdaran.

Before that, I had already been arrested several times during May and early June 1981 by members of the Committees, but each time I had got away after some insults and blows. On 8 June in particular, during a peaceful demonstration in Tehran, I had been the target of an attack by the Pasdaran who were mostly members of our neighbourhood committee and who knew me personally. They hit the demonstrators with coshes, knives, machetes and nunchakus. In the group that they had encircled, they cruelly hit the protestors, most of them girls and young women. It was during this attack that one of my friends, Tahereh Naghdi, who was later killed by the regime's agents in Evin Prison, was severely wounded. But finally, thanks to the people's help, we managed to break the circle and save Tahereh and the others.

On 14 June, because of having organised

book-stands in the street, we were arrested with my fellow team member, Sedigheh, after having had an avalanche of blows from the Pasdaran. For three days, the latter kept us in their cars which went round the streets of Tehran. They had put us, Sedigheh who was pregnant and me, between men who kept beating us incessantly for three days with coshes, their fists and their feet while driving through the city. Sedigheh lost consciousness. Knowing she was pregnant, I tried to serve as a shield for her to cushion the blows. My face and body were covered with bruises. At 11 o'clock at night, they finally led us to a Committee in the north of the city, named Vozara, and threw us into a cell until the morning. In that Committee, new cells had just been built. Ours were empty, without even a straw mattress to sleep on. We stretched out on the cement floor until the morning when they came to look for us, dragging us on the ground and throwing us into a car, under their feet, and started insulting and hitting us again as soon as it set off. They had beaten us so much that we could no longer find the strength to move. On the third day, at 10 in the morning, they flung us out of the car into an alley at the north end of Mossadegh Street, barefoot and with swollen faces. Seeing us in that state, some street traders, feeling pity for us, gave each of us a pair of *tongs*, which we put on before going on our way. We went to a friend who lived five or six bus stations away. She welcomed us warmly and prepared a meal after having heard our story. Not having eaten anything for three days, we gobbled everything up in a second. Then she took us to a doctor, a friend of her family. He dressed our wounds. The trouble was that, what with our wounds and the bandages we had on our faces, we were continually stopped and questioned by the Pasdaran.

On 18 June, when I was crossing a street, I was tracked down by some of Khomeini's men, who arrested me and shut me for two days in a Committee under the Seyed-Khandan Bridge. They threw me into a tiny room where they beat me up with butts of guns and coshes. They had used a cutter they found in my bag as an excuse to say I wanted to kill a Pasdaran. In the course of two hours, they got up a dossier in which they had put some *Mojahed* newspapers, some of the organisation's books and a kitchen knife covered in blood. They used it to interrogate me, asking me how many Pasdaran of Islam I had killed with that knife. During those two days when I had my eyes constantly bandaged, they took me several times to Evin Prison, saying:

"Now we'll send you to Hell. Our job is eliminating the Monafeghin (a pejorative term, meaning "hypocrite", used by the regime for the Mojahedin). And you, with that dossier, you're a good one."

They took me to various places, like the basement, where they hung me up by the upper body and made me listen to horrifying screams and howls of tortured people to drive me mad and force me to acknowledge the dossier.

It was the first time that I was personally confronted with torture. The biographies of martyrs of the Shah's time had alerted me on the subject. At the time when I was reading their memoirs, to resemble them was my finest dream. To be able to resist torture to liberate my people, and not to betray them, or their convictions, formed an ideal which I never thought I should one day have to confront. But the first time that I was taken to an unknown place, where I heard screams and howls, that I was hung up and hit, I began to tremble violently, terrified. I was afraid above all of not being able to endure the horrible tortures, of which I could only hear the victims' screams. I turned towards God to pray him to help me bear the pain and not lose the faith I had been to so much trouble to acquire. At night, in my nightmares, I cracked. I then woke up with a start, and sat for several minutes thinking: *If they come to look for me now to interrogate me, am I ready to bear it and not to give way?* At first, I felt powerless before my torturers, but then I realised that if Fatemeh Amini, Mehdi Reza'I, Badizadegan[9] and several others had held out in that situation, why couldn't I manage it

---

9. Famous political prisoners from the PMOI in the Shah's time, violently tortured then executed by the Savak, the political police.

too? Noticing that reinforced my motivation considerably.

Once, they took me into a cell on whose walls was written: "The pain of tortures disappears, but the shame of betrayal remains." Reading that, I began to tremble, saying to myself: *My God, let me not fall into the number of the traitors!* When I prayed and reached the sentence "Do not put me among the traitors and those who have lost the straight path", the sentence on the wall came back systematically into my head. But when I was whipped for the first time, I finally felt much less afraid. The fact was that I understood that, faced with the torturers, the determinant factor was one's own will. To decide, even at the price of one's life, to bear up or to give way. And I had decided to resist, not to yield.

Fleeing from my father's claws

After two days in that Committee, when they saw that tortures and blows were of no use, on 20 June at 11.30 a.m., they finally let me out of a car in Abbas Abad Street in

North Tehran and went away. If they had known that the Mojahedin were organising the historic demonstration of 500,000 people that day, they would never have freed me.

As I had wounds and bruises on my face, in the street, as I passed, the patrolling Pasdaran threw me glances of hatred. Two of them even called out to me, to ask me what brawl I had been in. They wanted to arrest me, but I told them that I had had a car accident two days earlier and that I was just coming back from the doctor's. That's how I escaped a fresh arrest and came home.

In the quarter where I lived, there was also a centre of the Pasdaran and the militia. As they still kept an eye on me, while I was on my way they stopped and questioned me. They wanted to know where I had been and why my face was in that state. I told them the same story. *It really was the last straw*, I told myself then: *those mercenaries, without the slightest reason or authorisation, hit us with unheard-of violence and bash our faces in, and not only can we not complain, but on top of that, those same wounds serve as an excuse for them to arrest us and torture us again, and it's up to us to prove that those aren't traces of torture!*

At last I reached home. As I came in, I caught sight of the tense face of my father, apparently furious because of my long absence. But when he saw me in that state, he said nothing to me. From his silence and his look, I realised that he had evil intentions. In the time it took him to put down the Qur'an on the ground and stand up, I ran onto the terrace, and by going from roof to roof, I managed to reach the last house in the street. I went in and explained the situation to the owner. Faced with my father's cruelty, she took me in her arms, led me into her house and served me some very hot tea. As my face was swollen and black with bruises, she didn't let me go out alone. She said that if those miscreants of Pasdaran saw me in that state, after what had happened that day and the demonstration that had turned into a bloodbath, they wouldn't miss me and God knew what they would do to me. That's why she kept me at her home for a time, then escorted me to help me leave the neighbourhood. She took me to the place where I wanted to go and then left. From that day on, I didn't go back home. So as not to fall into the hands of the Padaran, I slept at friends' or relations' houses every night, but I had to change my hiding place frequently because, after a time, no place was safe.

So, on 14 July 1981, as I had nowhere to go and the house of the friend where I had been living until then had been attacked by the Pasdaran, I wandered about the streets. That day, the Pasdaran pursued me several times. My brother, the one who worked at the court, wanted at all costs to arrest me and was directing the Pasdaran. I managed to escape several times, but as there was really nowhere I could go, after having wandered through the streets for hours, I finally took shelter after midnight with my aunt. An hour later, my brother arrived; all the evidence showed that he was looking for me. Once sure of my presence, he went out again. Half an hour later, while I was asking myself what to do, the Pasdaran surrounded the house.

They attacked with such violence and hit the door so hard with the butts of their guns that my old aunt, in a panic, fainted from terror. Once the door was open, the Pasdaran rushed inside, they handcuffed me and bandaged my eyes. They led me to Dadgostari Prison[10]. The day before, they had visited my father and arrested my sister Mahine, aged 45, a mother of two. At first, it was a matter of interrogating her in order to find traces of me and of Najmeh. But, in fact, she was serving to some extent as a hostage. They handcuffed her and took her to prison. Even after my arrest and that of Najmeh, they didn't release Mahine and they kept her for two years in the court's prison and then at Evin in the worst of conditions. Needless to say, her children remained with no one to look after them.

---

10. A prison attached to the Palace of Justice, reserved in principle for common-law prisoners.

THIRD PART

Captivity

In the machine shop

For twenty days, I didn't know in which prison I had landed. In fact, they hadn't thrown me into a cell, but in the machine shop, a very narrow, dark and dirty place, not even fit for an animal. That little room was swarming with insects and animals of all kinds, including mice and cockroaches. Stinking black water oozed out of the ground; the heat was stifling. What with the summer heat of Tehran and the gases and smoke from the machines, it was really intolerable. Besides, the working machines made a non-stop deafening racket. Even my screams of protest and my blows on the door couldn't be heard.

In that little room, I could neither sit down, nor sleep, nor eat. After two days spent without swallowing a morsel, I was thrown some food – I don't know what it was – in a greasy and dented iron box. By throwing me that pittance in a dog's bowl, they wanted to humiliate me and make me co-operate as soon as possible. I didn't touch that meal or any other during the week that I spent there. I only drank a little water from the tap from my hands. During all that time, very much weakened, I murmured repeatedly to myself: "I shall never collaborate with the enemy of humanity" and that gave me strength.

At the end of a week, the guards came to look for me and to take me elsewhere with my eyes blindfolded, with the aim of questioning me. They made me believe that it was a difficult place to reach. One of them took my hand, saying:

"Take care! You'll fall! Don't bump into the wall! Gently!"

Or else they exchanged words that terrified me, very quietly. For example, about the dismal fate that was awaiting me:

"Don't worry, they'll give you some water before your execution."

They played cassettes of howls and said:

"That's the fate that awaits all hypocrites! But if you want to, you can save your life!"

A little later, I realised that my sister Mahine was also in a little room not far from mine, and that she was questioned about me when I was I their hands.

After a series of interrogations, I was transferred from the little room to a cell in the same prison. There were, for example, prisoners incarcerated for trafficking drugs. The place was repulsively dirty. At the end of a week, owing to the lack of hygiene, I caught skin diseases and fungal infections. During the twenty days I spent in that prison, we weren't taken to the shower once. We had no spare clothes and the lack of hygiene was total. We couldn't even wash our clothes. We were covered in grease. When a girl fell ill, she very soon infected the others. Fungi were clearly visible on the skin. They had grown to such a size on my feet and legs that I could no longer walk. I had to sit all day with my legs apart to avoid the rubbing which worsened the wounds. The guards saw it clearly, but refused even to give me any soap. Every time I asked for some, they systematically retorted:

"Tell us first who you are so that we can know whether or not we can give you anything, you vermin. Because if you're a 'hypocrite', then go to the devil, and if you're not one, then you must say so!"

The old lady who was crying

Dadgostari Prison, as I've said, was reserved for common-law prisoners, who had been removed before we arrived. Opposite our cell a woman remained, with broken features and an unhappy air. She looked 70 or 80, while she was only 50. She spent her days pressed against the cell door, crying. I tried several times to speak to her through the bars. I asked her why she was there. She didn't answer and wept. I asked her in vain for her name. In short, all my attempt to approach in order to calm and comfort her resulted in failure. Her tears and lamentations tortured me. That poor old woman was alone at the end of a cell, and nobody was paying her any attention. Once a day, a guard came to bark the worst of insults at her, shouting:

"Dirty old sniveller, you'll stay here until your death! You've lived too long already, that's your punishment unless you answer."

After innumerable attempts, she finally answered me. She said:

"My little girl, nobody believes me, why should you?"

I went on insisting. Then she told me:

"My son-in-law resigned from the Committee and as he supports the Mojahedin, they accused him of theft. They accuse me of having helped him escape and knowing where he is. I've been here four months now, and my son-in-law has run away. I'm being insulted and humiliated as you can see. They want me to tell them where he is and they'll let me go. In four months, they've only taken me to the shower three times and all my body's eaten by vermin."

Transfer to Evin Prison

Finally, at the end of August, I was transferred

with my sister Mahine, who was seriously ill. We were thrown into a car, and covered with blankets so as not to see anything outside, and led to Evin where we were led straight to interrogation. That day we were kept waiting until the middle of the night to be questioned. After several hours, we earned a quick interrogation to ask us for our names and addresses. Then we were put in Section 240. This section consisted of three rooms. One was reserved for the royalists, who had everything a prisoner could need. They were buddy-buddies with the Pasdaran and got whatever they requested. The other two rooms contained the rest of the prisoners. 70% were schoolgirls and students and 30% teachers, doctors, nurses and officials. Each room, 5 x 3m square, was crammed with fifty to seventy people, without the guards transferring anyone.

There were also little schoolgirls, whose first names I remember: Farzaneh, 11 years old, Forough, 12, and Zahra, 15. Their crime? Supporting the Mojahedin. In fact, these children had been taken hostage until their sisters or brothers, their fathers or mothers gave themselves up. Farzaneh and Forough were so young that they fell asleep during their interrogation or else, when the Pasdaran shut the door and wouldn't let them go to the lavatories, they couldn't contain themselves.

On 27 September, a rumour circulated that the Mojahedin and the demonstrators had attacked Evin Prison. As a reaction, the guards shut the cell doors for three days, not letting anyone out, even to go to the lavatories or perform ablutions before praying. In a room 15 metres square, where fifty-five people were piled up, what could be done for those three girls who couldn't contain themselves? We lifted up the moquette in a corner of the room and put down an iron box, so that they could use it as a chamber pot. Of course other people used it too. At the end of three days, the air had become unbreathable. After many requests, and at the price of blows and fresh interrogations, they opened the day and let us go to the lavatories.

One Pasdaran, who was called Alizadeh, was the head of the section. She bore a particular hatred for the Mojahedin. She humiliated and insulted those little girls in the worst possible way. She used to hit them, shouting:

"You deserve it! The imam said we could loot everything that belongs to the hypocrites, goods, money and women. I couldn't care less what happens to you. You must all be slaughtered. You're not wanted!"

That's what all Khomeini's supporters thought. That's how Zahra, who was 15 years old, was executed on 12 September 1981, after six months of torture[1]. She had stated: "I am a Mojahed," refusing to repeat "I am a hypocrite" as Mullah Guilani had ordered her to do. The radio announced the news of her death that same morning.

Mullah Mohammad Guilani, a religious judge and president of the Supreme Court known for his cruelty, ordered the execution of one of his sons and the pursuit of another who was assassinated by the revolutionary

---

1. Zahra was arrested in the spring of 1981. The People's Mojahedin hadn't yet begun their resistance, but the powers were doing all they could to suppress them. During the two and a half years that preceded 20 June 1981, fifty PMOI militants were assassinated in the street by the regime's gangsters and over 1,500 languished in political prisons.

guards.

I had no more news of the fate of Farzaneh and Forough, who had been transferred elsewhere shortly afterwards. But I shouldn't be surprised if they too had been executed, as that criminal Guilani hadn't hesitated to declare in a radio and television broadcast watched by millions of viewers, in response to the protests against the execution of children aged 12 or 13:

"A child aged 9 lunar years for a girl, and 15 for a boy, is considered a major and therefore can be executed."

When I was transferred to Evin, as I was covered with fungi, the girls in the cell did everything possible for me to have a shower every day, even in cold water, in order to care for me as fast as possible. The hot water only ran for ten minutes a week and was normally reserved for girls whose feet were in a very bad state because of torture and whose pain would have been aggravated by cold water. The others, in spite of the icy temperature of Evin, washed in cold water. When we spoke of it to Hassani, the executive director of Evin, he answered us that we must thank God and that if we complained too much, our water would be cut off.

Evin is an immense prison complex built during the reign of the Shah of Iran for political prisoners, situated in North-West Tehran at the foot of the Alborz range which dominates the capital. Khomeini's regime developed it, going so far as to transform the administrative block into cells. For example, in the north part of the complex, 400 isolation cells were built on four storeys by the prisoners undergoing hard labour in 1983. The guards in the mullahs' prisons are Pasdaran who fulfil at the same time the offices of guards, interrogators and torturers. They use the repenting prisoners and the traitors as Kapos.

Brother and cousin torturers

Because we're speaking of Hassani, let me tell you here that he was my cousin, his real name being Abolfazl Hadj Heydari. He's the nephew of Askar Oladi. He is considered to be his pupil. In the Shah's time, he had spent a few years in prison with Askar Oladi and Assadollah Lajevardi. He had been freed by the Shah like Askar Oladi, Lajevardi and Karoubi[2] who all acquired positions of high responsibility in the mullahs' regime. As a response to being freed, they all appeared on television shouting in chorus "Thank you, King of Kings", before being released. For their liberation, they had promised the Savak (the secret police) to pursue their war against the Mojahedin even more assiduously. Abolfazl Heydari had a great influence over his brother Aziz Jadj Heydari and over my elder brother Mohammad Hadj Heydari. He took them to the court and to Evin. Hassani was the prison's strong man. As to Aziz and Mohammad, they did the torturer's job: cowled, they tortured under false names.

When I underwent an interrogation, it happened that I realised if the principal interrogator and the one who stood above me were Aziz (my cousin) or Mohammad (my brother). For, from their questions, one

---

2. Mehdi Karoubi was twice president of the Majlis, the mullahs' parliament. An unsuccessful candidate in the presidential election of 2009, he is one of the conquered faction in the regime's internal conflicts.

could see that they had detailed information on the family. Once, to be sure, I lifted my blindfold at the right moment and I saw that traitor Aziz. On his side, he saw that I had recognised him and, to punish me, I was whipped and tortured for a whole week.

From September 1981 onwards, the arrests were increased and the prison's maximum capacity was reached. The number of prisoners in each section was above the norm several times, so much so that not one more could be added. The air was unbreathable. They were obliged to take us into another section which was also called 240. As usual at Evin, the sections were on two storeys. I went to the upper one, my sister Mahine to the lower. Each floor normally had six rooms. To understand better in what conditions we had lived, it's as well to make it clear that the population of the three rooms where we had formerly been entirely filled the twelve new rooms. When the transfer was complete, our old section was turned into an infirmary.

After our transfer, the section head told us one day that a delegation consisting of the director of the prison and of his collaborators would come and see us. We were all sitting in our cells. I was in number 1 when Hassani, the head of the prison, who was part of this group, put his head through the door. All my doubts were confirmed, I had confirmation that this torturer was Abolfazl, my cousin. I was shocked, and bearing the same name as that criminal disgusted me deeply. We had nothing in common, and well before I had joined the Mojahedin, I had kept my distance from those members of the family because of their savage and corrupt behaviour. Full of arrogance, he looked me straight in the eyes:

"Who are you?"

I too looked at him and didn't answer. He repeated his question.

"Azam Hadj Heydari."

Then, with an insolent smile, with an oily laugh, he asked me:

"What have you done?"

I said nothing. He reiterated his question, but then I looked straight into his eyes without answering.

The girls complained of not having

enough water for the shower, that it was icy and that there was no hot water. With the same smile, he said to them:

"Thank Heaven that you have some water!"

In answer to the girls' various requests concerning basic needs for hygiene and food, he simply answered with absolutely anything.

A torturer's true face

You are no doubt curious to know how a torturer behaves in his normal, family life. In the preceding pages, I have tried so far as I was able to speak of the icy and distant relationship that my brother Mohammad maintained with my mother and my sisters. I think that he felt hatred for all women, even us. A hatred which came straight from Khomeini's ideology and with which he was impregnated to the marrow of his bones.

Before Khomeini's coming to power, Mohammad was already one of his fierce adherents, but he still remained, like many people, within a certain norm. It was that ideology that made him into a monster capable of torturing and killing his own sister without the slightest after-effects.

He looked just like Lajevardi . He wore traditional shoes, a simple collarless shirt, fastened with a button. His clothing was simple, he wore a beard and always carried a rosary. His head bent, he tried to wear a very humble, wretched air, detached from life. But it was a farce. Behind that demagogy, he hid the black heart of a criminal who had made a fortune.

A young sprout

While I was writing down the way my brother had actively participated in my arrest, I remembered a girl I had been very fond of, also a victim of the lack of affection caused by Khomeini's ideology, because she had been handed over to the regime's agents by her father.

In September 1981, when I had just arrived in Section 240 at Evin and didn't yet know the others very well, I saw a girl come in, aged 16 or 17, tall, pleasant-looking, with a firm and decided step. In spite of her young age, her face and personality attracted everyone. I looked at her for a long moment, then I stood up and went towards her. I introduced myself and asked her name. She answered calmly, with a warm smile:

"Atieh Moharer Khansari."

I asked her if Tahereh was her sister, and that was so.

In fact, I had already seen her once or twice with Tahereh, when she was younger. How she had changed in two years! I asked her why she was there.

"Because I love freedom," she answered me.

I laughed:

"That's our common denominator."

She indicated the other girls and said:

"It's the common denominator for all of us."

I appreciated her sense of repartee. When I asked her how she had come to be arrested, she sighed:

"It's my father! When I came home, he handed me over to the Pasdaran."

After that, we became friends, because of those points in common, of Atieh's exceptional qualities and her personality. I felt very close to her. Atieh was really an extraordinary girl. Her kindness, her affection, her devotion to the others, made her, in spite of her youth, a source of support for many prisoners.

In our section, there were three rooms, one of them reserved for the royalists with whom the women guards didn't let us communicate. In the two others a hundred and fifty people were piled up. That's why many everyday tasks, such as washing one's hands, going to the lavatories or even sleeping were nearly impossible. In those conditions, solving the problems as best one could meant putting other people's interests and needs before one's own. One needed a to be big-hearted for that. That's how we were able to evaluate Atieh's good qualities. She was 17 years old, but she was as patient and solid as a rock, firm and full of rage against the Pasdaran, the traitresses and the spies, and her determination in the struggle escaped no one. She was like a mother to the girls in the cell and tried to fulfil their material or emotional needs, to the point of forgetting what she needed herself. She comforted those who felt lonely or downhearted and covered them with attention and tenderness. That's why she seemed much older than she really was.

During the transfer of the prisoners from the court to Evin, of which I was a part, because of the catastrophic hygienic conditions, we had brought with us some lice which we had transmitted to many other people, as well as fungi and dermatological infections. Moved by the greatest patience and tolerance, Atieh helped all the girls, specifying that serving them gave her pleasure. For example, she could spend whole mornings scrupulously delousing the girls, then she hugged them and said those were the sweetest moments of her life. She loved them with all her heart and all her soul and truly nurtured them.

Atieh left for and came back from interrogation with the most total calm, like an experienced resistant, a Mojahedin who had known all the difficulties and joys of life. She let nothing that had happened appear and came back to the cell with a joyful air.

She demonstrated a particular serenity which was a source of comfort for me. Her dignity and solidity filled me with pride and honour. She was an exact reflection of her sister Tahereh. The latter, in the first few weeks that had followed 20 June 1981, had been tracked down by Pasdaran who had wounded her when opening fire. Transferred to Evin, she had died under torture. Atieh embodied order and discipline, she overflowed with love for her fellows, demonstrating affection, kindness and assurance.

There are truths that one sometimes finds it hard to accept. Atieh's execution is one of them. Neither I, nor any of the girls wanted to believe it. But who could have believed it? She was so young, she had done nothing! There was nothing in her dossier. She had been arrested only a few days earlier … But at midnight, on 14 September, they called her to her interrogation. My heart seemed to stop beating. And suppose she was going to be executed? Suddenly the whole cell was quiet, as if everyone was trying to convince themselves that she was really going to be interrogated.

Hardly had Atieh left the cell when my heart started beating madly in my chest. My eyes were glued to the door. Every time it opened, I jumped. I counted the seconds and prayed that the door would show Atieh appearing. But nothing happened. Finally, at 4 in the morning, the dull sound of machine-gun fire pierced my heart and invaded the prison. Everyone in the cell held their breath. We didn't know how many people had been executed. A heavy silence fell. I felt as if my heart would tear my chest apart. We waited for all the fatal shots to be fired. When they began, we started to count them, our throats tight. One, two, three … and the shots went on. That morning, in that bloodstained dawn, we counted up to sixty. And then silence fell again. Had one of those bullets been fired into Atieh's head? I wept inwardly: *But how could they have cut down that child? My God, for what crime? Just because she passionately loved freedom?* Yes, that was enough for those criminals. I remembered her words. The common denominator of those sixty innocent people who on other nights reached a hundred, sometimes two hundred executed, that was it: a wild love of freedom, so wild that they were ready to pay for it with their lives.

I don't know whence came the voice that broke the deathly silence that weighed like lead on the section, but suddenly a song arose in which we all joined in chorus:

"Mojahed, Mojahed,
Mojahed be faithful to your duties
It's you who embody the hopes of the people
It's you the flame that lights tomorrow's way."

The song over, we fell into one another's arms, hugging one and another and swallowing our tears. But I stayed awake until the morning. I was lying down, unable to close my eyes. I still hoped that Atieh would come back. I suddenly felt a hand fall on my shoulder. It was Shouri[3] who was lying beside me.

---

3. This was Dr Massoumeh Karimian, who was executed, and whom most of the prisoners nicknamed Shouranguiz, or the diminutive "Shouri". This great lady and doctor was, according to tens of testimonials, a mountain of resistance and tenacity in Khomeini's prisons. She was born at Karbala in Iraq and had studied orthopaedics in Germany. She worked for the Iranian Red Crescent and was imprisoned from 1981 to 1988, the date of the slaughter of political prisoners, when she was assassinated with 30,000 others.

"Azam! You're not asleep?"

"No, I'm waiting for Atieh, she hasn't come back yet."

We stayed on the alert until 6 in the morning, with no news of Atieh. All of a sudden, the door opened and I thought it was her. I jumped up, happily, and ran to meet her, but no, it was a mistake. It was her cousin that they had taken away with her. Then I knew that Atieh was one of those executed. But I still asked:

"Where's Atieh?"

In silence, she looked fixedly at a point on the ground, then said:

"Atieh sang 'Mojahed' then she went away."

What a coincidence! In the section, we too had sung that song.

The end of an escape

A month after that incident, they introduced a dozen spies and traitresses into the section, three in each cell, to watch over and report the deeds and actions of the most resistant in order to frighten us and make us passive.

One of them, Homa Gassemlou, who knew me personally just as she did some other girls, was charged with the job of catching us. She followed us like a shadow. She watched everything we did, sleeping, speaking, eating and all the rest. Even when we were waiting our turn to go to the lavatories or the washbasins – as their number was insufficient and gave rise to queues of twenty to thirty people – those spies joined the queue to check on our conversations.

One day, I was looking at the fine line of sky that showed between the bars on the window. It was our only diversion and the only place in the section where we could exchange a few words, even some information, with the girls in other sections. The mound that we saw from the window was called the hill of death. At night, a powerful floodlight lit it up. Often, there was a very bright star just above it. While I was absorbed by that landscape, Homa the spy arrived:

"What are you looking at like that? Get away from there!"

"Why? It's a crime, then?"

She repeated it twice, three times and began to threaten me.

"I don't give a damn, do what you like!" I shouted at her.

While I was duelling with her, I suddenly realised that someone was climbing up the hill on all fours. I didn't take my eyes off him. A prisoner had managed to escape his guards and was doing everything he could to reach the top. I heard my heart beating. If he was tracked down, it was the end of him. Had he a chance of getting out? I didn't want to lose a second of that fight between life and death. Then two shots rang out; at the third, the prisoner collapsed. A few moments later, the spies who were pursuing him reached his level. He was no longer moving. They took him by the arms and legs and took him away. I never knew what he was called, or how he had been able to escape and get as far as that.

Traitresses worse than the Pasdaran

After our transfer to the new section, it didn't take long before, with some new arrivals, we were over 400 prisoners. Now the maximum capacity was 100. At night, given the lack of space, I slept with many others in the corridor. But because of the many comings and goings, and the prisoners who went to be interrogated, we didn't manage to sleep. So we sat up and talked until the morning or else, secretly, we did some manual work.

In the first few months of 1983, practically every night, between 3 and 4 in the morning, fifty people on average were executed and, every night, we heard the shots being fired. Suddenly, the crackling of the Kalashnikovs tore the night apart, then silence fell again. A second volley of fatal shots rang out, giving the number of the dead, and the whole prison then fell back into silence.

But the worst was when, a few minutes later, while we were still in shock, the door opened and traitresses like Homa Ghassemlou and Faranak Majidi came in. They disgusted me profoundly, and still more at those precise moments. They threw cruel looks around and repeated the psychological tortures that they had learned, laughing:

"Why are you looking at us like a lot of

frights? Oh yes, we've been to finish them off, so what?"

At those moments, it was harder to bear their words than to hear the fatal shots. I had the feeling that claws were being driven into my skin and that all my nerves were being pulled. Anger and hatred took me over

To such an extent that I really struggled not no jump at their throats and strangle them; but I was reduced to silence. We could only throw looks black with hatred at those apprentice torturers, who were even more detestable than the executioners. By creating that nervous tension, they deprived the prisoners of sleep by making it impossible for them to go to sleep again. They harassed us much more than our torturers did.

How to resist

The Pasdaran wanted to weaken the prisoners, not only physically, but also and above all by annihilating their resistance and their struggle, and destroying their humanity. That's why they did all they could to separate us and then to break us separately, because they had understood well that our resistance was the result of the groups we formed. On our side, we were always thinking of the way to stay together, to give one another strength, hope and confidence.

A girl suggested one day that each of us should give a talk on a town, her own or one she knew. We must speak of everything we knew about that town, its history, its culture, its traditions, its dialect or its language, its economy, its social life, etc. That project was warmly welcomed and we called it "The Journey to the Towns of Iran". Some of us knew really interesting things about their towns. Mahdokht Mohammadi-Zadeh, for example, told us about Kerman. It was so precise and pleasant that I said to her;

"Mahdokht, it's as if I were there. If I go to Kerman one day, I can visit it with my eyes shut."

The day she was executed, she said to me:

"Azam, if one day you're set free, don't forget Kerman and don't miss its marvellous starry night."

Then with a warm smile, full of kindness,

she hugged me and went away.

Another conference subject was the sciences. All those who had acquired knowledge from their studies

or their private reading had to give a lecture about it. Once, while I was talking to Zahra Nazari, I told her I was interested in biology and the evolution of the Earth and of life.

"Ah! I did biology at university and I used to adore it."

"Used to? Why, don't you like it now?"

"Yes, but a stronger passion's replaced it, the passion for freedom that I found in the ideals of the Mojahedin. You'd like me to give courses in biology and evolution?"

"Oh, yes! But you're being interrogated at the moment."

"Forget that!"

Every day, she gave me a two-hour course in the history of evolution and life forms, like a true professional, mastering her subject without books or notes, thanks to her memories. It was so fascinating that I remember her teaching quite clearly over twenty-five years later.

Zahra felt a deep love for the prisoners and thought she had a true responsibility towards them. She had endured cruel tortures for long periods, but never let anything show. She never spoke of the tortures nor of her resistance. We had heard girls bear witness to her courage and her strength, to the way she made her torturers powerless and how they had been incapable of getting a single word out of her.

In this way, in that hell, whose conditions were comparable to what we had read and heard about the Nazi concentration camps, strong in the support of those revolutionaries, thanks to those deep human relations and that common ideal, we knew some great moments.

We understood well that it was necessary to keep our spirits up at all costs and not let the enemy attain his goal, which was to break us and deprive us of all hope. So as to keep our spirits up, we did manual work: we made things with our hands from the minimum of materials we had at our disposal in prison.

For example, by pulling coloured threads from their worn-out clothes, the girls made some very pretty embroideries. We used everything that came to hand, such as date stones or bones for example. We let the latter whiten in water for a very long time, then we filed them by rubbing them or engraved them with pebbles found on the way when going to interrogations and picked up secretly in the yard. We sculpted them to make statuettes or pretty pictures. Everything was a sign of resistance and perseverance.

Our activities drove the torturer Lajevardi and his spies raving mad. They tried by means of blows, tortures and threats to stop us doing whatever. Many prisoners had an empty or almost empty dossier. But they underwent great pressure because of that kind of resistance, and many, for that reason only, became the prey of the torturers' anger and hate and paid for it with their lives.

In our section, there was a great spread of social levels: schoolgirls of 14 or 15, graduate students, doctors, officials, housewives. But that diversity didn't cause divisions or quarrels.

On the contrary, everyone tried, with what they knew and with their strong points, to help the others. The common quality of that diverse group was good humour, good spirits and strength. Exactly what the torturers and traitors couldn't bear. They couldn't, however, avoid recognising it and tried, by insults and other forms of vileness, to stop the girls being cheerful, or separated those who were a little older. But it never worked.

Joy and gaiety

We transformed the routine moments, the difficult and stressful conditions in the prison, into subjects for joking in order to spend some happy moments. Showering, for example, was an event that was turned into a special day, full of noise and laughter. On Tuesday, there was hot water. Giving everyone their turn and defining priorities were difficult tasks that needed tact. There were always twenty or thirty girls who had been severely tortured, with open wounds whose pain would have been intensified or that would have been infected by cold water.

They therefore had no choice except to wash in warm water. The person responsible for taking turns sent them off first. Then came those who were old, weak and ill. Most of the girls showered in the icy water of Evin, up in the mountains, where even in summer it ran cold from the pipes. Needless to say, in winter it froze us to the marrow.

But in spite of everything the girls had managed to make the shower a treat, and enjoyed it with a great deal of noise. We all went there together, counting: one, two, three! We then rushed under the jet and washed at top speed. Those are things that nobody, I think, could do alone. In a group, not only did the fear of the cold water fly away, but washing like that became a kind of struggle and an entertainment. That was how our bodies learned to resist. We adapted ourselves to showers in icy water and no longer caught chills as easily as we had at first.

The meals, breakfast, lunch and dinner, were unspeakable. But the girls had made them a happy moment. They had nicknamed the cart that brought the food "the happiness carnival" and we savoured our tiny, inedible portions with so much laughter that it made hell bearable. The torturers and spies who witnessed those scenes went mad with fury as none of their pressure contrived to break us.

Sport was an appreciated activity that raised our spirits. Certainly it was forbidden, but three times a day, morning, noon and night, we did it in secret. According to circumstances, we formed groups of thirty to forty or else of ten to twelve people, to do exercises. Sometimes, when conditions worsened, we practised individual activities, each on her own, in the lavatories, the showers or in a corner, far from the eyes of the Pasdaran or the spies. At the end of the movements, when we were together, we formed a circle and, when possible, we took one another's hands and chanted a slogan. And if conditions didn't allow it, we contented ourselves with shouting "hurrah".

Every day, the torturers elaborated a plan to break us. We too put together a counter-attack and always found a way to neutralise them. One of the actions on which the torturer

Lajevardi particularly insisted was to take the prisoners into a room called "Hosseinieh" to film them and show them on television. In that way, the powers made people believe that all the political prisoners had abandoned the struggle, had repented and converted to Khomeini's Islam. In spite of all his threats, all his blows and his whip, Lajevardi only managed to take a small number of the prisoners into that room. Those who went there did so only to exchange information with the girls from the other sections.

The first time I participated in that circus was during the Ashoura ceremonies in 1981. The men and women were sitting in rows, separated by a curtain one metre high. In this way we could see each other, and many girls were looking for their brothers who, they knew, were also in prison. The programme began and as soon as the cameras began to roll, the women pulled their chadors over their faces to such an extent that not a single prisoner's face appeared. As to the men, they had pulled their hats down over their eyes and lowered their heads. Impossible to film such a scene, everyone would have understood. Lajevardi had to intervene. But he couldn't tell the women to take off their chadors or show their faces. He insulted the men, telling them to take off their hats and raise their heads.

"Sons of …! You who always stand upright, how is it that here you lower your heads?"

Seeing him so furious, we rejoiced.

That day, they gave us as much tea as we wanted. In general, nobody drank it because it was full of camphor and the very smell of it was nauseating. We had therefore decided to bring back as much sugar as possible to the section. In prison, sugar is precious because in the absence of food and anything strengthening, we gave sugared water to the girls who were coming back from torture or who didn't feel well. Everyone therefore brought back as much sugar as possible in her clothes. On reaching the cell, we emptied our pockets and filled a bucket. For us it was a real victory. The second victory was the stories that everyone told about Lajevardi and his troops who had been baffled and the anger that gnawed at them. We went over them, laughing, for days on end.

When we first arrived in Section 240, the torturers brought us, as they said, "by mistake", prisoners who had been filthily tortured. They had martyred them with such barbarous methods that in spite of being used to witnessing that kind of scene, we were shocked.

One day, at nearly 3 in the afternoon, while I was walking in the corridors, they brought in a woman on a sort of stretcher. Her body was entirely covered with bruises and she was so swollen that she was twice her normal size. Those who knew her told us she was Parvine Kouhi[4]. Seeing her in that state, I couldn't hold back my tears. I wanted to go and speak to her, but she had lost consciousness. Shortly afterwards, the section's loudspeakers came on, repeating several times:

"Parvine Kouhi to the section office."

But Parvine was unconscious. She could

---

4. After a few years in prison, Parvine Kouhi was freed and rejoined the Mojahedin. She now holds a position of responsibility in the Resistance

neither hear nor move. Finally, some Pasdaran
came to take her away; they themselves had
made a mistake in taking her to the communal
section.

Another time, the door opened and a
new arrival came in. As she had just come
from the torture chamber, she came forward
bent double, with great difficulty. Sunburnt,
tall and with broken features, she seemed
pleasant and attracted one at a first glance.
I went towards her; her feet were shredded.
She looked me full in the face and laughed. It
seemed to me that I knew her, but I couldn't
place her. She said to me:

"Azam, don't you recognise me?"

I was ashamed that she should recognise
me and that I couldn't manage to do so myself.
She laughed again pleasantly, saying:

"It's me, Sima, have you forgotten? It's
not your fault, my face has changed, but I'm
still the same."

She reminded me of two or three places
where we had militated together as teachers
supporting the Mojahedin. And suddenly it
all came back to me.

"It's not true, Sima! It's you? I can't believe it!"

It was Sima Hakim-Mahani who had aged ten years in one. We had worked together before 20 June 1981. She was the only daughter of a fairly well-to-do family and had studied at the university. She had never lacked anything, but she had chosen to fight and until the end she remained faithful to her convictions. Her legs were in shreds, her wounds were purulent and the infection had reached her blood. To revenge themselves for her resistance and her refusal to capitulate, her tormentors gave her no treatment so as to torture her even more. They finally took her in that state to the execution squad.

Another of those heroines was called Shahrbanou Ghorbani[5]. She had been tortured with such violence and hatred that her face was unrecognisable. Nobody could recognise her and her arrival in the section had overwhelmed everyone present. From the tortures she had endured, I realised how

5. Sharhrbanou Ghorbani, member of the PMOI, was born in Semnan. She was a student of natural sciences. She was executed on 20 September 1984, at Evin Prison in Tehran.

noble and precious her humane ideals wer, to give her a limitless capacity to tolerate pain and make such a hard fight easier.

At the end of three days, they took Sharhrbanou away and we didn't see her again. It was about a year later that I learned of her death, but I know neither where nor how she was executed.

Facing the traitresses

After some time, I became part of a group of girls transferred to a new section. I soon realised that I knew everyone. Some girls had been taken away for interrogation, others because they had refused to speak, and we hadn't had any more news of them. After having gone all round the section, I was so happy to see them again that the shock of having left my friends in the old section disappeared. As I had thought that many of them had been executed, finding them there, alive, in front of me, was a real gift from Heaven. Parvine Ha'eri, Maryam Golzadeh-Ghafouri, Homa Radmanesh, Azam Taghdareh were there, like many others. They were all condemned to death. But why had they been regrouped? Perhaps in order to make them break under the pressure of the executions. But that plan didn't work either, because none of the girls yielded and they were all executed.

Parvine Ha'eri was a strong girl, well-known for her incredible resistance, both physical and mental. The traitresses and torturers knew her determination and her personality well. The girls had nicknamed her "colonel" because of her great height and her firmness, which had the gift of enervating the spies and the recanting women.

Hourieh Beheshti-Tabar had a master's degree in economics, a topic that she taught with particular passion to her fellow-prisoners, doing all she could so that they shouldn't have an idle moment.

Her activities had attracted the thunder and lightning of the Pasdaran and every time they saw her, they insulted her. This attitude and this perpetual hatred made us understand the importance of her rôle. Everyone loved Hourieh. She was about 45 at that time. She had very poor eyesight, about 2/10th. The

Pasdaran and the traitresses covered her with insults drawn straight from the uncultivated vocabulary of the mullahs. At least twice, on a filthy, lying pretext, that is to say some so-called deviant conduct, they stretched her out on a bench, and, under the eyes of the other prisoners, savagely whipped her.

Another prisoner was called Homa Radmanesh. The torturers couldn't bear her. She was extremely tiny and didn't weigh more than 45 kg. But she had a solid, strong personality, was patient and tolerant, and felt much love for all her fellow-prisoners. Never did we see on her face a trace of sadness or defeat. This strong point produced a visceral hatred towards her among the regime's agents. They said she acted in secret and under cover. In fact, Homa's mere presence, valiant and generous, in a cell or a section boosted the climate of resistance and raised the spirits of the other prisoners.

As soon as we arrived in the section, we entered into conflict with the local traitresses. We protested, asking why they were there and why they were guarding us.

We were prisoners and we wanted Pasdaran and official guards. But the regime wanted to confront us with traitresses and hide behind them, to say that the prisoners were fighting among themselves. To protest, we had started a hunger strike, as we had at Evin, calling it the "thirteen-day strike".

It began when the traitresses brought us a meal and we refused to take it. We said that we didn't accept those guards. None of us touched her meal and the next day they took it away and brought another. Day after day, it began again. This confrontation which went on under a rain of blows and multiple attacks from the traitresses (supported by the guards and the Pasdaran) continued. They brought a meal and put it down in front of the section door; and we, as a form of protest, touched neither the meal nor the tea, and didn't answer any of their requests. So it lasted for thirteen days and some prisoners, including Homa, fell seriously ill. Having been unable to stop our strike, the torturers moved seventeen prisoners. First to the infirmary and then, two weeks later, to another section.

A kid of 13

Towards the beginning of 1982, because of the large number of arrests, the overpopulation in the section became such that every day people were fainting because of the pressure and the lack of air. This caused many displacements of prisoners and we were taken to a bigger section.

One day, while I was sitting near the door of Cell 1, I saw a kid of 12 or 13 come into the section. Looking careworn and worried, her eyes red with tears, she came towards our cell. But suddenly she stopped dead at the door and looked at us with astonishment without knowing what to do. I knew that state among the new arrivals. It was peculiar to those who had just been arrested or who arrived after a long period of solitary confinement. I went towards her.

"Good morning! Don't worry, come and sit down beside me."

"But where are we?"

Her answer stopped me short. What did she mean? Didn't she know she was in Evin?

"Come and sit down, come on, rest a bit

113

and then I'll tell you."

She was very tired, she was hungry and thirsty. Unfortunately, we had nothing to give her. We therefore went from door to door in every cell and found a little bread in one and a little rice and lentils in the other. She took a few mouthfuls before breathing:

"Ah! I was ravenous."

She was called Fatemeh and it was clear that she was lost. She didn't speak correctly. After talking with her a little, I understood that she hadn't been to school. She came from the town of Saveh, south of Tehran, with a completely empty head. She cried and asked for her mother.

"But how did you get here?"

"My father's in the Committee and he has a workshop making candles. He works there with my uncle. One afternoon, it was shut, and a boy in the neighbourhood came. He told me he wanted to do something and asked if it was possible to do it in the studio. As he was also one of the family, I let him in. But the Pasdaran said he had explosives. When the Pasdaran came, I helped him run away. And it's my father who handed me over to the Pasdaran."

She cried and said she wanted to go and join her mother. That evening, we tried everything to calm her and we found her a place beside us for her to sleep. Next day, the loudspeaker spat out her name for an interrogation. She was trembling with fear and wouldn't stop crying. She asked where they wanted to take her. I took her in my arms, saying to her:

"Don't be frightened! Be brave! Nothing will happen to you."

I hugged her and she went to be interrogated. When she came back, her feet were covered in blood and swollen, and she was unable to walk. She came into the section and fell to the ground, head first. We picked her up and helped her to lie down. Her mind wandered and she cried out:

"No, no, let me go!"

In spite of our searches, we couldn't find any food to give her. When teatime came, about fifteen girls didn't take their sugar so that we could give her some sugared water to help her get her strength back. After a few hours, she came back to herself.

"Where are we?"

"In the cell, you were asleep."

"It's not still the interrogation?"

"No, don't be frightened! We're here … Fatemeh, when you were asleep, you were shouting: 'No, let me go!' What happened?"

With her eyes full of tears and a lump in her throat, she told me.

"You know … They'd put me in a corridor. Some men came and they started to laugh and then to bother me, very dirty, you see … In my sleep, I thought they'd come back."

When Fatemeh finished, I couldn't keep back my tears. My God, I thought, what has that kid who doesn't know how to put one foot in front of the other done to fall into the hands of those wild beasts, without being able to defend herself? Then I realised that one couldn't expect anything else.

"Listen, if they come back, you too have to hit them and defend yourself."

"But I'm not strong enough," she

answered me in astonishment.

"It's not important whether you're strong or not, the what's important is that you should defend yourself."

Suddenly she smiled as if she had just understood something.

"Come on, we're learning something here! Next time, I'll defend myself."

In the cell, Fatemeh had become friends with Helene Arfa'i. Pretty and full of life, Helene was a schoolteacher aged 22 or 23. But she looked much younger and was like a schoolgirl. Under her influence, Fatemeh grew a little stronger and braver every day. When the traitresses saw that in a few months Fatemeh had gone from being a simple, illiterate kid, who during the first days didn't even know how to talk, to being a courageous and combative girl, they took her to what they called the "court". They had said to her:

"You're being freed because of your father who's a soldier of Khomeini and works at the Committee. Go and thank your father who sent you here to be educated. The lashes you've received were for the sins you committed in the past. Go and thank God and don't tell anyone anything, so that you won't be used against Islam and the Imam [Khomeini]."

When she was freed, she still had the wounds on her feet.

A mother tortured in front of her daughter

The interrogations began on the day of my arrival at Evin, and every day brought its allowance of new situations. One day, when I was waiting in the corridor to be interrogated, I felt that a man had sat down, pressing himself against me. I told him to move, but he didn't listen and didn't answer. I reiterated my request several times, with no result. I finally raised the blindfold over my eyes a little to see who it was and what was the problem. How surprised I was! He was dead. I looked at his face. I knew him, I had seen him before. I thought a little and remembered that I had seen him in a Mojahedin office. He was called Reza Mashadi.

I was still in shock from seeing Reza's body, when I noticed that the interrogator was in front of me. He immediately thrashed me violently. The blows sent me spinning against the walls and the people round me and, as my eyes were bandaged, I couldn't control myself and fell. After that avalanche of blows, they took me to Block 2 for my interrogation because I had raised my bandage.

"So, as you're so fond of seeing hypocrites going to Hell, come, peel your eyes, perhaps you'll go and join them too."

When they took me into the block to hit me, I heard the screams of a child of 5 or 6 who cried without stopping. I very quickly understood that she was seeing her mother being whipped. I heard the torturer say to her:

"Tell me your mother's name and I'll stop hitting her."

The little girl was called Fatemeh. But I never knew whose daughter she was. Later she was transferred with her mother to Section 209.

27 September 1981 in prison

One day, I was called for interrogation and

taken into the corridor of a block where I was made to sit down. Nothing happened. No interrogation. I saw a lot of people around me, sitting squashed against one another and then, a few minutes later, they disappeared. I asked myself what, frankly, was happening. Where were those people going? In order to know, every time they came to look for people, I changed my place so as not to be taken back to the section. Several times, a little old man who was bringing people and taking them back passed down the corridor, shouting my name, but I didn't answer and so I spent the night down there. At one point, when the room filled up again, I asked one of those lads:

"Who are you?"

"What difference does that make?"

"What's your name?"

"I've just been arrested."

"But why?"

"Because I participated in the 27 September demonstration."

"The others too?"

"But who are you?"

I introduced myself.

"I've come from Section 240. I'd so much like to know where they're being taken."

"They're all going to seal with their blood the commitment they've made before God and the people."

"Could you tell me a bit more?"

"Well, I'm telling you and no one else, they're all going to be executed. It's with shouts of 'Long live Rajavi, long live freedom!' that they're joining Hanif and the founders of the Mojahedin."

After a few minutes, Ismaël, my interrogator, who had seen me talking with the prisoners, threatened me and in that tone typical of Khomeini's hooligans, said:

"In a few minutes, all your pals, with songs and stamping their feet, are going to see each other in Hell."

I stopped breathing. So those groups of fifteen to twenty people who at the beginning of the evening came and went after one another in the corridor, were all being taken away to be executed? I was still in shock, when the interrogator shouted:

"Haji, bring me that hypocrite, it's not her turn yet." And then, addressing himself to me: "So you've understood? Next time, ask me."

When that damned Haji brought me back and I passed right next to the prisoners who were lined up, I counted them, looking from underneath my bandage. There were forty-five of them. My legs wobbled and my heart beat madly. I wept in my heart: Lord, but how is it possible that they execute them without having interrogated them and without even knowing who they are? Many of them, as the young man beside me had explained, had been arrested in the street just for looking suspect. When I came back to the section, quite a lot of girls were awake and I could see easily that they were anxious. They asked me where I had been and why I had come back so late. What had happened? I really didn't want to talk. But when I saw that they insisted, I explained to them that there had been no interrogation and that I had feinted. Then they started to laugh but were surprised to find I didn't join them. Simine

Hojabr asked me in astonishment:

"Azam, what's happened? Why aren't you laughing?"

Then I told them everything.

Towards 2 or 3 in the morning, I went to lie down without being able to sleep. I was thinking, when suddenly shots broke the silence of Evin. I held my breath. The fatal shots began, one, two, three … There were over fifty shots. Silence fell again. I turned round, everyone was awake. I was still in shock when Simine began to sing a song from Lorestan[6] in her sweet voice. I thought she was lying in her place and was singing from there. When I turned round, I saw that she was stretched out just behind me. She had come closer and had found a place. When she had finished, she said to me:

"Azam, I've sung that song just for you and for all those who've gone. I'm very happy."

"Why?" I asked her in astonishment.

"I'm happy because I'm going to join them soon."

"Stop, don't say that, couldn't you say

---

6. A province in West Iran.

something else?"

She had such a sweet, grave smile. She went back to her place. A storm was sweeping my heart.

We never cried in front of the Pasdaran, the guards and the traitresses at the time of the executions. But that evening, I hid my face under the blanket and cried in silence for all the innocents who had been shot and for Simine who, I knew, would soon join them.

The girl who laughed

Simine Hojabr was a pretty young girl of 16 or 17, with matt skin and a sweet voice. Her family came from Lorestan, but she had grown up in Tehran. She had been arrested because of her support for the Mojahedin. She had a steely mind, one would have said she didn't know what fear was. She was a real lioness. She spent every day at interrogations where she was systematically whipped. She had, as they said, her daily "ration". But when she came back to the cell, as soon as the door opened and she put a foot inside, she began a song from Lorestan in her warm, laughing voice, as if nothing had happened. Once, I told her that because of the way she came back, starting to sing and laugh at once, they would hit her harder. She would do better to stay silent for a few minutes. She answered me, laughing:

"They're sticking their fingers in their own eyes. I'm the one who's going to win, whether I get a hundred blows from a cable or a thousand, I'll go on singing."

One day when I had gone to be interrogated, I saw a girl who came from another section and whom I knew. She was waiting too.

"Azam! Is Simine in your section?" she asked me.

"Yes."

"You know she's a lioness. One day she was whipped for two hours and when they took her out, to make her sit down beside me, she was smiling. She asked me if I'd had my 'ration' too. I said, what's the 'ration'? Then she told me that every day she had her 'ration' of lashes, like the grub. First she swallowed the lashes, then she went back to the section to have her meal. Haji, the torturer, came to say to her: 'With all you're getting, doesn't it break your spirit?' and took her away."

Everyone knew her because, wherever she went, she spoke to everyone to get information.

Her gaiety influenced all the girls who loved her very much. Her big brother, Cyrus Hojabr, had died under torture in a prison in the north of the country, at Sari. One of his shirts had been brought back to her as a souvenir, and she wore it all the time and kissed it saying:

"I'm proud of my brother, he kept his promise and so shall I, I've taken my decision."

The torturers didn't take Simine away from Section 240 to execute her straight away. First they sent her round by Section 311 where they tortured her violently for a month. It wasn't so as to obtain information, but to avenge themselves because she had never yielded. However, right to the end, she stayed faithful to herself, she fought like a lioness and her name is engraved forever in our collective memory.

One morning, after having heard volleys at dawn, the radio announced the names of those executed. Simine Hojabr was one of them.

The radio wasn't transmitted by the loudspeakers except to give the names of those executed. Afterwards, the guards turned it off. Those imbeciles thought they would break us with those announcements. But they didn't know that every time the names of those Mojahedin men and women were announced, we renewed our commitment. That day, when Simine's name fell, the girls decided to organise a ceremony in her honour. We prayed and distributed cakes in her memory. The recollection of Simine, the brave one, firm as a rock, modest and kind, remained very vivid in me, as if she were by my side. We learned things about her when we made some research years later at the research centre on the martyrs[7] where the souvenirs of the prisoners are collected. Such as, for example, that she had been a highly motivated pupil at Hashroudi

----

7. This means a museum of the Resistance in Ashraf City belonging to the PMOI in Iraq.

School, that she had been very serious in her activities, but that her smile never left her.

She had been arrested in August 1981. And in spite of the large amount of information she had, she didn't say a word. On the eve of her execution, they brought her back to a cell near ours. She said aloud to a mother in her cell that she was going to be executed that evening or the next day and she asked her, when she was liberated, to take the shirt back to her mother as a souvenir.

"Look what they've done to my feet, my arms, my face and my body, but I'm still afraid that I wasn't able to act as I should have."

It's reported that Mrs Javaherian, who spent the last night with Simine, said that her whole body was covered with wounds and that she had no nail on her big toe.

On the afternoon of her execution, she had begun to recite the Ashura[8] prayer, and had sung "Kiss me"[9] in her fine voice. She had talked and laughed so much that everyone

8. Religious mourning celebrating the death of the third Shi'ite Imam, Hossein, the Prophet's grandson, assassinated by the ruling power of the period.

9. A celebrated song about a father who asks his daughter to kiss him before going to the execution squad.

looked at her in astonishment. And when they called her, she said with a smile:

"Be seeing you, bye bye!"

Evin: the tragedy of 8 February 1982

In the evening of 8 February, while talking in low voices among themselves, the Pasdaran and the torturers threw insults at us. They had taken me to Section 209 to identify a sister in the struggle, Siba Sharifpur. I was standing in the corridor of 209 when I saw the agents behaving in a completely unaccustomed way, coming and going and whispering. Suddenly, in the middle of their conversation, they started to laugh, a scabrous laugh, saying that there was something to celebrate. I felt the pressure grow and asked myself what was happening. I tried to see something of what was going on from underneath my blindfold. They brought me back to my cell, saying they had finished and that they would come back later to fetch me. Then, mockingly:

"Let's let her go and see her pals to celebrate with them."

I spent that evening in anguish because

all the agents, everywhere, were laughing and mocking while constantly trying to get at us. To those who were coming back from being interrogated, it was clear that all the blocks were bathed in the same atmosphere. The interrogators laughed and said they had to distribute cakes. And all the girls were asking themselves what was going on.

It was the next day, when we learned of the death of Ashraf Rajavi[10], of Moussa and their comrades, that we finally understood what all that carnival was in aid of.

The mullahs who thought they had finished with the PMOI had deposited their bodies in the yard of Section 209, on a heap of earth, with the idea of breaking down the prisoners. They had put us in rows, forty

---

10. Ashraf Rajavi had a responsible position among the People's Mojahedin; she was also the wife of Massoud Rajavi, the historically important director of the Resistance. She had a baby a few months old when she was assassinated by the Pasdaran. Moussa Khiabani, number 2 in the PMOI, was with her in the same house with seventeen other Mojahedin when the attack was launched. The only survivor was Ashraf and Massoud's child whom Lajevardi hastened to exhibit on television, standing above the lifeless body of his mother, and promising to make him a fervent partisan of the regime. This scene aroused general indignation in Iran. The child then spent a few years in prison, then was rescued by his paternal grandparents, before joining his father abroad and becoming part of the resistance on reaching adulthood. He is now in Ashraf Camp in Iraq.

by forty, to go and see them. Lajevardi held Mohammad, Ashraf's baby, in his arms, above his mother's body, with a cruel laugh. He wanted to demoralise the prisoners.

They thought that the Mojahedin were dead and that our resistance would come to an end.

On Lajevardi's orders, the bodies of the heroes had been placed so that their heads rested on an unstable pole. So as to be sure of making the prisoners suffer more, he kicked one end of the pole to raise the heads. He suddenly withdrew his foot, the pole fell back and the heads on the lifeless bodies knocked hard on it. Lajevardi then laughed his fetid laugh, yelling:

"Come and see your martyrs, how they hold up their heads, how they've been reduced to nothing!"

He looked straight in everyone's eyes to gauge them. He wanted to apply as much pressure as possible. He burst out laughing:

"Today it's our feast-day and your day of mourning."

But everyone looked at him with such

hatred that he finally lost his poise.

He also viciously demanded that the prisoners should insult the martyrs. But most of the lads and girls saluted them with respect and spat in Lajevardi's face. A gesture they paid for with their lives in front of the execution squad.

In this way, the demonstration of force that the regime had wanted to give to weaken the spirits of the Mojahedin prisoners and the other members of the resistance did the opposite and stimulated them. So much so that the project of making all the prisoners pass in front of the victims' bodies was stopped short.

The echo of 8 February 1982 in the sections

When the news of the death of Ashraf and Moussa was announced on the section's television, nobody believed it at first. Then a heavy silence enveloped all the people present. Nobody spoke or moved. Parvine Haeri, who had just come from being interrogated and hadn't heard the news, contrary to her usual smile and good-humour that nothing could shake, seemed to have grasped the extent of the catastrophe. She stood right in the middle of the room, pale, uneasy and anxious.

"Parvine, what's happening to make you so uneasy?" I asked her.

"It's for you to tell me. Why this silence everywhere?"

She was right. In fact, the silence was the law of the Pasdaran. That was why the section always had to bustle about and be active. But that day, at that precise moment, everyone looked stricken. However, that silence didn't last. It was Dr Hajar Robat-Karami and Fatemeh Assef, who were the oldest, who broke it. They came out of their room saying that silence was what the regime wanted to announce that it was all over. Parvine, who was silently walking up and down the corridor, ran towards them to say she agreed. Those three girls, who were later executed, broke the silence. It was Hajar who started by reciting the Ashoura prayer. She sang more loudly when she reached the verses saying "I am the enemy of your enemies and the friend of those who love you". Very quickly the ice of the first shock changed to a fire of roaring hatred that inflamed all hearts. The girls redoubled in affection for one another. I felt that we had become the links in a chain, joined to one another. Nobody could have separated us.

The torturers had filmed the scene of the martyrs in the yard of 209 to show it in all the sections, with the intention of breaking down the prisoners. But each transmission gave rise to an explosion. Everyone ran out of the cells, the rooms and the corridors to see the heroes' bodies. The girls sang a hymn, wept, clasped one another in their arms and swore to continue on that path, without bending, to the end, a path in which Ashraf and Moussa had sacrificed their lives.

A wave of executions

After the prisoners' stinging response to the tragedy of 8 February 1982, the torturers revenged themselves by redoubling the violence of their tortures and interrogations. Hate and vengeance reigned at Evin.

Mahdokht[11] remained under torture for two whole days. Just like Fatemeh and Zahra Samimi-Motlagh, whose ordeal lasted several days.

When they summoned Farah Torabi, Fatemeh and Zahra Samimi, then Zahra Nazari and Elaheh Orouji, everyone knew what awaited them. They too knew that they were going to be executed. When they heard their names, they ran to perform the traditional ablutions before their martyrdom.

I shall never forget Zahra Samimi-Motlagh and her innocent face. She displayed her sweet smile all the time. One would have said that she had always heard good news. She accepted all events without being disturbed. When she was summoned to her execution, she preserved the completest calm. She had

---

11. Mahdokht Mohammadi-Zadeh, a student of orthopaedic medicine, was the person responsible for medicine in the section and took care of the sick with great abnegation. In the research centre's documents on the martyrs at Ashraf City, I found in the memoirs of a political prisoner a passage concerning her in which she said in particular: "One day in prison I was talking to Mahdokht and Soudabeh Rezazadeh. Mahdokht wa saying: 'How I should like to go into the villages of Iran and in all the remote places that lack everything, especially to go and help the children, give them schooling, so that they learned to distinguish their friends from their enemies.'" Mahdokht was executed in July 1988 at Evin prison during the slaughter of the 30,000 Mojahedin political prisoners.

that smile on her lips. We all took her in our arms and kissed her, weeping. When it was my turn to say goodbye to her, and she saw all my tears, she said to me:

"But Azam, it's not a bad place to which I'm going! Why are you crying? I've chosen the best destiny there is and how happy I am that it's reaching its goal! I hope to be able to fulfil my responsibility to the end."

With these words, she said goodbye to everyone. Hadj Khanom (Mrs Tavanian Far) brought the Qur'an so as to make them pass underneath it. They kissed the Qur'an and left joyfully, with smiles on their lips, as if they were going on a beautiful journey.

Norouz, New Year 1982

At the New Year – *Norouz* – 1982 (21 March in the Persian calendar), I found myself in Cell 1 of Section 240. A few days earlier, we had decided to prepare a Norouz celebration with the means available. We had all gathered to check the resources we had at our disposal and decide what could be done with them. In general, we prepared something we called

"Soukht-Jet" (aviation fuel), for the girls who came back from torture, to give them some strength. The girls, laughing, suggested preparing aviation fuel for everyone. And what would happen if for once we all flew off together? We decided, first, to obtain the sugar. So everyone went off to look for something in a corner of the room. We surprised ourselves with our finds, given the conditions we were living in: dried figs, dates and even some powdered milk. We even unearthed a tiny bit of chocolate in the lower section. Thanks to the fairy fingers of Parvine Haeri who had a very keen sense of taste, we concocted two kinds of cakes, one which resembled nougat and some kinds of dry biscuits. In the middle of each cake a salted chickpea was enthroned, and we signed them with the name of a celebrated Tehran pâtisserie. We had devised them far from the eyes of the spies and traitresses. When the section gathered together, we put them right in the middle of the prisoners. With what pleasure we savoured them and how we talked about that first production of cakes in prison!

Who's the "hypocrite"?

In spite of all the torturers' efforts to stop us holding that celebration, we had a *Norouz* celebration in Cell 1 of Section 240, just as they did in all the cells where Mojahedin prisoners were to be found. In our cell, we celebrated with a few folk dances, including a Kurdish dance and one from Azerbaijan. While a young Kurd was performing one of her regional dances for us, suddenly some Pasdaran women, including the notorious Alizadeh, erupted into the section. They seized our dancer's beautiful hair which came down to her waist even though she had cut it in prison. Alizadeh rolled it round her hand and tried to pull the Kurd out of the cell in that way so as to hit her and lead her to the torture chamber. That immediately aroused a wave of protests on our part. On the one hand, there were those three Pasdaran who were pulling her, and on the other, all the prisoners. The Pasdaran had to give up in the face of our fury and our numbers. But we were well aware that they wouldn't leave it at that after such a stinging defeat and that our gesture would cost us dear. However, in spite of whatever might happen, we were all satisfied, because we had pulled together: it wasn't just one girl who was involved; the guards had to punish a great many prisoners. And that's what happened. Only a few minutes after the Pasdaran had left, the loudspeaker summoned fifteen girls to be interrogated. We knew that punishment and very hard blows were awaiting them. The prisoners who had been called only came back two days later. They had been interrogated and tortured in a more than barbarous way during the whole of those two days. When they finally came back, they were covered with blood and wounds, with their eyes sunk deep in their heads. Their faces had turned yellow. The Pasdaran Alizadeh opened the section door and pushed them inside. In a vinegary voice overflowing with that particular hatred she felt for the Mojahedin, she mocked:

"You hypocrites, if you want to amuse yourselves, just start that Norouz celebration again!"

"We all know who's the 'hypocrite," I shouted at her, not wanting to let her have the last word.

She looked me straight in the eyes and left. I knew what was awaiting me. Very soon, the loudspeaker spat out my name. They took me to 209 for the interrogation, my eyes blindfolded, and left me to hang about in the corridor, where every passing Pasdaran and interrogator gave me violent kicks and punches and sent me spinning against the wall.

To humiliate me, those obsessives seized the chance to feel me up; and when I resisted them, they rained blows on me. Some of them pressed their dirty mouths to my ear to whisper insults and filth drawn straight from the mullahs' twisted culture, with yelps of oily laughter. When I reacted to the attacks of one of them, he said to another:

"That rabid bitch must be tied up so as to calm her a bit."

Then they tied my hands behind my back so that I couldn't go on defending myself against their attacks. They did that to me for a whole day and, at 2.30 in the morning, they brought me back to the section.

In the eyes of those inhuman torturers, joy, laughter and group work were the signs of "hypocrites". That unpardonable crime must be punished in the most savage manner. The Pasdaran couldn't stand the slightest movement on our part, and execrated the mere fact that we walked.

"A Mojahedin doesn't gripe"

One day when they had taken me to the interrogation block and I was the target of sexual harassment, I said to one of them:

"But haven't you a mother or a sister, and yet you behave like this?"

Suddenly, he went mad. Bawling, he took off and jumped with both feet on my stomach.

"I've a mother and a sister," he bellowed, "but not like you, you w[hore]!"

The effect of the blow made me feel that my intestines were going to come out through my mouth and I really thought I was going to

141

die. I lost consciousness. I don't know how long it lasted, but after a time, when I came to myself, I was still bent double with pain and shaken with violent nausea. I started to resent God. But where art Thou? *But what art Thou good for if thou lettest us be oppressed like this? Why doest Thou not answer them?* I was lamenting when the agent arrived. He pulled my chador, took me away and threw me into a cell in 209. I was lying in the cell, bent double with pain. I talked to myself and addressed prayers and complaints to God. Suddenly, coming from the wall next to me, I heard a noise. I knew a little Morse.

"Who are you?"

"Massoumeh! What are you doing?"

"Nothing. I was complaining to God about those torturers and griping because I had no one to talk to."

"A Mojahedin shouldn't gripe. This is a way that we have chosen."

I was silent. I felt ashamed of my reaction to the disgusting way that my torturers had behaved to me and that the mullahs use to break a woman down. That sister's few words had a great effect on me. She gave me a lesson in resistance and patience. But later, however much Morse code I tapped, she no longer answered. Surely she must have been taken to be interrogated, for no sounds came from that cell any longer. When I went back to the section and asked my fellow-prisoners who that Massoumeh was, they told me she was Massoumeh Azdanlou.

Massoumeh had been arrested on 2 April 1982, after hours of resistance to the armed attacks of the Pasdaran in the quarter of Tehran where she lived. She had been wounded and had lost consciousness. The regime had announced first of all that she had been killed in a confrontation but, in fact, from the start, she had been put under torture. Four bullets had hit her: in the neck, in the jaw and in the arm. Shortly afterwards, she could no longer walk, and it had become very hard for her to speak or eat.

The report that Fataneh Avazpour wrote of what she had seen of Massoumeh and what I was able to read in the documents I found later in the research centre on the martyrs, give the following details: *"At the moment of her arrest, Massoumeh was severely wounded. She was pregnant, but they made her undergo the worst of tortures."*

Nahid Izadkhah-Kermani, who was her sister-in-law and who had been able to see her in her isolation cell in Section 209, specified that her face had changed so much that, at first, she hadn't recognised her. At the end of June 1982, by mistake, instead of taking her to 209 the Pasdaran had sent her to 246. They had taken her to Cell 3 in which was Zari Nahidpour, a friend of hers from the University of Science and Industry, to whom Massoumeh was very close. She had therefore run to her side and acquired some scraps of information about what had happened. Massoumeh had breathed to her:

"They want the address of my sister Maryam[12] and all the important information I have about her. They know I have it all, but I'm going to hold out to the end and I won't give it up."

As long as Massoumeh hadn't come to

---

12. Maryam Rajavi, now the President-elect of the Iranian Resistance.

246 and Zari hadn't spoken to her, everyone thought she was dead. The Pasdaran soon realised their mistake and brought her back to 209.

During her imprisonment, the torturers spared Massoumeh no barbarous ordeal. All that cruelty was aimed at making her speak on television and repent in public. Finally, on 30 September 1982, when she no longer had the strength to walk, speak or eat, and she could no longer move her neck, they sent her in front of the execution squad.

Breaking the prisoners by accusing them of depraved morals

As all activities and collective movements in prison were forbidden, the Pasdaran found excuses every day to cosh us and create a climate of terror. They couldn't stand our demonstrations of joy.

One of their miserable methods of breaking down the prisoners who resisted them consisted in accusing them publicly of sexual deviance. That's how, one day, they brought a bench into the section and set it down in the middle of a room. They read out several names including Zohreh Ainolyaghine and Razieh Ayatollahzadeh-Shirazi before announcing that they were going to whip them in front of everyone present. Hourieh Beheshti-Tabar stood up, saying:

"If you want to whip and torture, do it, that's your job. But it's intolerable that you should whip us while accusing us of sexual crimes. You've sunk very low!"

Surprised by those unexpected words, the Pasdaran retorted:

"So you've done the same thing too!"

They threw themselves on her like hyenas so as to rain blows on her. Under torture, Hourieh had practically lost her eyesight and wore glasses. They were shattered into fragments under the blows and poor Hourieh could see nothing any longer. The Pasdaran laughed at her, throwing her to left and right like a ball. Their scabrous laughter drove us wild. Hourieh alone kept her countenance.

After having attacked her like that, they stretched her out forcibly on the bench so as to whip her. However, Hourieh's dignified behaviour, just like the way they had treated her and transported her, had given us courage: we all turned round then, against the wall, as a sign of protest. Nobody wanted to see her comrade being beaten. Faced with this collective reaction, the torturers went mad with rage. They summoned the special forces commanded by one of the most terrible torturers in Evin, Majid Halva'i. That "gorilla", as we nicknamed him, alighted in the section with his group of twenty or thirty Pasdaran cosh-wielders. Supported by the traitresses, they beat us up and rained punches and kicks, blows from cables and coshes on us, so that we should end up by turning to face the bench and watching our friend being flogged. Although they beat us for two whole hours without stopping, although, under the violence of the blows from the coshes, several prisoners had their bones broken and some fainted, they didn't achieve their aim. We brought them to their knees.

A girl's sad story

From the events of that period, I insist on

telling the story of this young girl which is one of the saddest and at which I happened to be present. These events are forever engraved in my memory. One night, when I couldn't manage to sleep and was walking up and down, I glimpsed a kid I didn't know, as she was new. Her silence and calm had attracted my attention. She was tall and extraordinarily beautiful. Deep sadness and grief veiled her face. That night, I saw her walk up to the sleeping prisoners. I decided to go towards her, especially as her behaviour, at this hour, intrigued me. Her hands on her hips, she seemed to be looking for someone. She stopped in front of every girl, bending forward to watch her face, then passed on to the next. She couldn't be more than 16 or 17. I started to follow her and watch her. Suddenly, she bent towards a girl, then she seized her throat so as to strangle her. Horrified, I intervened by holding off her hands. I took her in my arms, I begged her, I hugged her, trying to move her away and speak to her. She quickly recovered her calm. Squeezing my hands with all her force, she put her head on my shoulder and cried for a whole hour. A few girls woke up, like Maryam Golzadeh-Ghafouri, her potential victim, and Azam Taghadareh. They threw me a glance and made me a sign I didn't understand, before going back to sleep. If they knew her, if they had seen what had happened, how could they go back to sleep without reacting? Her behaviour had shaken me profoundly and I tried to make her speak. She was called Nadereh. This child of 17 had watched the rape of her sister Tahereh, who had been tied to the cell's heater. She was looking for her sister among the prisoners and couldn't find her. Suddenly she thought she was in front of the rapist and tried to strangle him.

Judged!

In spring 1982, they finally took me to the "court" for my so-called judgment. The judge, Mullah Mohammad Guilani, was one of Khomeini's well-known torturers. They had brought as a witness an enormous Pasdaran with a monstrous face. I think he was there to frighten us. The trial – a few words, a lot blows and an even greater number of insults – only lasted ten minutes.

FOURTH PART

Two worlds confront each other

Lajevardi's theory

It was already 1983. The longer it went on, the more the repression was intensified with the aim of breaking down the prisoners who were still alive and, as they said, "closing the chapter of the Mojahedin". Lajevardi had a theory that the Mojahedin resisted so long as they were together. If they were separated, each one placed in isolation, at the end of a year there would be no more prisoners.

He deplored the prisons' lack of dungeons in which to isolate all the prisoners. He had therefore imagined ways of making the conditions of captivity even more difficult by transforming the communal sections into isolation cells. Consequently, all contact between prisoners, even a good-day, was considered a crime. Mutual help, especially, was totally forbidden and every violation led to the cruellest tortures and punishments. That's how the "last judgment" section emerged in Ghezel-Hessar Prison[1], equipped with cages and coffins, of which I shall speak later. In a word, Lajevardi wanted to empty the Mojahedin of their humanity. It was with this aim that they invented horrific permanent tortures such as the cage, the coffin and the residential unit. They wanted the prisoners to conclude finally that all group work, all collective life and contact with someone else was the source of evils, ordeals and pressure.

If you wanted to undergo your punishment, you had to do it all alone like a sheep.

If your friend or someone else was killed before your eyes, you must not react.

But the experiment showed that

---

1. Ghezel-Hessar Prison was built under the Shah's regime in the town of Karaj in the suburbs of Tehran. Consisting of three departments, each containing 2,000 prisoners. Since 1981, two departments have been reserved for political prisoners.

Lajevardi didn't know the Mojahedin. We had discovered – I should say almost by instinct – that in that hell, our physical survival was tied to our collective life. Similarly, if, in spite of all that pressure, we survived, it's because we didn't give up our communal life, that is to say our humanity. With their cruelty that went beyond the limits of bearability, the torturers could make some of us crack, but they couldn't break us *all.*

They laboured to drive it into a prisoner's head that she was alone, that nobody was thinking of her, that she was forgotten by everyone, that her voice didn't reach anyone's ears and that her friends, to save their own skin, had accused her, her, of their own crimes. So it was useless to resist and doing so would only lead her to destroy herself. But the simple fact of feeling that she was not alone, that hearts in the prison or outside were beating with hers and for hers, gave her strength to resist. That's why we did everything communally. Sometimes we only had one apple, but we cut that apple up into ten or fifteen parts and all ate it together. It was the same with sugar, for example: every day, we were given a lump of sugar for our tea. Well, the girls kept those lumps, and put them together in one place so as to give sugared water to those who came back very much weakened from being tortured. As well as the physical benefit that a piece of apple or sugar could bring, above all it was positive from the moral and mental point of view both of the individual and the group. The simple fact that the victim of torture, faced with that wave of difficulties, pressures and torments, didn't feel alone and without succour, made her hold on. She knew that if she left to be tortured, if she fell ill, if for years she had no visits, people would continue to support her and defend her from the enemy's blows, to take care of her and nurse her.

As well as the grief and the pressure caused by the violence of the ordeals, those who cracked couldn't resist the psychological warfare conducted by the interrogators. They cut themselves off from the group and found themselves alone.

The torturers were really aware of the

force that the group provided. That was why, on noticing the slightest gesture of attention among the prisoners, they went mad. They saw what they had spent hours destroying with their lashes sprouting again because of the affection that the prisoners felt for one another.

Gohardasht Prison

Our group, which had been transferred from Evin to Ghezel-Hessar for punishment, underwent interrogations every day. One day, at 10.30 at night, one of Hadji Davoud's assistants, a sadist called Ahmad, came to the section door and gave my name to one of the traitresses that we had christened *Gestapo*:

"Tell her to get ready for a transfer quick and wait in front of the section."

When I wanted to get my things, Ahmad the sadist said to me:

"Don't take anything, you don't need anything to go to Hell."

Then I left the section with empty hands, in the cold.

Until the middle of the night, I was

kept in the interrogation room. During all that time, my guards kept shouting horrible things at me, such as:

"Don't be frightened, you're going to Hell, that isn't frightening. Make your will. Actually, you hypocrite, what's your will? Giving your sugar to a hypocrite and your lunch to another hypocrite who's been tortured and your dinner to another one?"

Their laughter was oily and vicious. I realised how much the humane feelings that animated our relationship exasperated them, and that made me proud. It must have been between 3 and 5 in the morning when Ahmad the sadist came and took me away, alone, in a Peykan car. He was the one driving it. During the journey, he didn't stop saying:

"Make your will! Sing us much as you like! Say all the prayers you can for the other hypocrites because there won't be any tomorrow! You've only got two hours! Do whatever you want!"

They lugged me about for hours through the streets around Ghezel-Hessar, making me believe I was the only one being transferred, while I could see other cars following us. Then they started hitting me, howling:

"Say what you've done! You haven't arrived yet and they want to send you back to Evin, why? Give us the name of your hypocrite accomplice and you'll be saved."

We arrived at daybreak in a prison that I couldn't identify. Everything there was new, only just built. As my eyes were blindfolded, I held onto the wall while climbing the stairs, and that's how I felt that the building wasn't finished. The floor wasn't finished either and my feet stumbled on earth, stones and rubbish. I understood afterwards that it was Gohardasht Prison which had just been built. A site opened under the Shah and finished under Khomeini. They filled up all its cells, which numbered one thousand.

In those cells, we heard no sound all day long. What terrified me was that I felt alone there. The section's Pasdaran were enormous men, of monstrous appearance, whose looks overflowed with hatred, savagery and unkindness. I didn't feel safe for a moment, either sitting down or asleep. During the two months I spent in that punishment prison, I was always on the watch. I always kept all my clothes on, whether for going out into the corridor or sitting down in a corner of the cell. Sometimes, I had the feeling that someone was watching me, behind the cell door. The guards all wore basketball shoes in order not to make a noise walking, to surprise us and behave obscenely. But I had learned to perceive their footsteps. I then looked fixedly at the opening in the door. In that way, when the guard showed up and eyed the inside of the cell, seeing me awake dissuaded him from coming in. However, once or twice, a vicious Pasdaran came up to me and had to leave because I started to howl.

After about twenty days without the slightest hygiene, the Pasdaran who was guarding me shouted at me:

"Hypocrite! To the shower!"

"No need!"

Then he came in, insulting me, caught me by my chador and took me to the shower, where he threw me into a cabin.

"You're doing that so that people should

say you're not being given showers!"

Without answering, I stayed upright in a corner of the cabin and didn't move. After ten minutes, I heard footsteps. Fear overcame me. An enormous man, bearded and hairy all over, with bulging eyes, arrived. He opened the cabin door, and, with a lewd laugh, he said to me in a vicious tone:

"Hypocrite, I'm scaring you? But why? It's your bosses who ought to scare you!"

He came in and drew near me. He clapped his hand over my mouth, lifted me brutally and took me into another cabin. There, in spite of all my efforts to defend myself and of my blows, he lay down on me and did everything he wanted. While I was struggling, punching him in the face and howling, he gave me two violent punches on the head and left. After half an hour, another one arrived:

"You don't want to wash? Then go and fuck yourself! Break up and rot in your cell."

I understood that the Pasdaran had made a pact: they came, they assaulted and raped me, then they didn't come back for a long time. Then it started again. It happened three times during those two months' internment in Gohardasht. One day when my eyes had been blindfolded and I couldn't see anything, a bloke I didn't know came to interrogate me in the cell:

"So do you still want to be a Mojahedin or are you sorry? If you don't, I'm going to make you sorry."

One evening, I heard a delicious voice singing, intoning the Qur'an and speaking aloud. It was addressing Ashraf, Moussa and other martyrs. She cried, she laughed, she prayed, she entreated the Lord. I was overwhelmed. I asked myself who it was. She wasn't afraid to sing or to speak very loud. Once, I asked her:

"What's your name?"

"Mehri."

"Why did they bring you here?"

They say I'm mad, but it's they who drove me mad. They rape me every day and they torture my sister and ..."

While Mehri was speaking, suddenly, that sadist's footsteps rang out and he took her away. I didn't hear her voice again and I never knew who Mehri was.

At the time of my imprisonment in Gohardasht, the prison hadn't yet been filled with floods of prisoners. When I looked outside, through the grille of my cell, I saw male prisoners who were being taken into the section opposite. After a month, I also heard the voices of women prisoners and gradually Pasdaran women joined the section's prison staff. A few days later, I left for Ghezel-Hessar.

The cage

In February 1984, I was in Section 7 of Ghezel-Hessar. The cells there had been planned for one or two people, but there were twelve or thirteen of us, sometimes even more. The cell was a little longer than a bed and 70 cm wider than the three-tier bunk bed that was in it. With the dozen girls shut up inside, it was difficult to sit down. Every day the guards found a pretext for punishing us by shutting the door. In order to sleep, every night, we had to solve a mind-bending puzzle. Several slept on the width of each bunk, with our upper bodies on the bed and our legs hanging. Those who were tall were a little more comfortable than the small ones, because they wedged their feet against the wall in order to sleep, but the little ones found it very hard to manage. Some slept under the bed in the opposite direction to the girls who were on top, their heads and busts outside and the rest of their bodies under the bed, and another two girls slept on the side. Obviously, when the door was open, all that wasn't necessary: then the girls slept all over the corridor and everything went a bit better.

In the corridors as well, we slept like sardines, stretched out on our sides. In that little space, the Pasdaran and the traitresses spent the night above us so as to make sure that we didn't talk to one another. If they reported that two people had talked, they went to be interrogated so as to confess under torture what they had said.

At Ghezel-Hessar too, once a week, there were twenty minutes of hot water. That day there was an atmosphere and, for the two or three hours when the girls went to the shower, before and after, the section hummed like a beehive. The person responsible called each of us in turn so as to respect the right order. Then we ran towards the shower as there were only twenty minutes of hot water for two hundred people.

Some prisoners were allocated the preparation of tea with the hot water from the shower: they held an iron box in their hands, in which they infused tea without camphor for those who were coming back from the bath. Every cell had someone responsible who prepared the cheese tin, washed it, and as soon as the hot water was announced, they all ran towards the taps to fill them with steaming water and make tea for the cell. If we missed the hot water, we could write off the tea. In that situation of total repression, all the girls were happy and laughed. Everyone appreciated that bathwater tea. The prison tea contained so much camphor that it accumulated at the bottom of the glass and we couldn't smell the tea, but as to the tea we made, it really tasted of tea!

The guards couldn't stand the climate of gaiety that animated the girls. They tried to break the ambiance with insults, shouts and sometimes even blows.

One day in February 1984, when the water arrived, we wanted to make the tea as usual. We had filled the tins and wrapped them in a blanket. In our cell, I was sitting with some girls on the third-storey bunk when suddenly the voice of the woman nicknamed *Gestapo* rang out.

"You're not allowed to make tea," she howled.

On the evidence, she was looking for an excuse because until then she hadn't said anything about tea. Nobody paid any attention and we went on as if nothing had happened. We were waiting for the tea to infuse when *Gestapo* came down, beside herself, to the prison guards' office.

After twenty minutes, the door opened and twenty-five girls, including Hengameh Hadj-Hassan[2] and myself, were called to

2. Author of *Face à la Bête* (*Face to Face with the Beast*), published by Pi-collec.

interrogation. Now Ghezel-Hessar was a prison for expiating punishment and didn't have any interrogation rooms. We all got ready and left the section. We waited for an hour in the guards' place. Standing up, I asked myself what they could make us undergo. Where would they take us? To Evin? To 209? To 311? To Gohardasht? I was afraid that they would interrogate us on what we were doing in the section: we hadn't agreed on what to say if we were interrogated. I remembered that sentence on the wall: "The pain of torture disappears, but the shame of betrayal remains." I implored God not to let me lose my honour as I had heard people speaking of what was called the residential quarters, the interrogators' new tortures concerning the organisation of the sections and I had also seen some of the results. *Lord, if I show weakness and I betray, make me die quickly. I do not want, in order to stay alive, to fall into the mire of betrayal.*

Fifteen of us were sent to Section 8, which was an isolated section, with a few more restrictions. We were taken, four other girls and I, into an unknown place. Hadji Davoud, the chief torturer at Ghezel-Hessar, told us, with an unpleasant look:

"I'm going to take you to a place like Hell, it's the day of the last judgment. You'll stay there till death or until you return to reason, choose to live and repent. You must say you were whores, that you were looking for a brothel and that you found it in the hypocrites' organisation and joined it."

Hadji Davoud, with his ignoble laugh, his inhuman monster's face that made him into a gorilla, went on:

"I'll keep you here until your hair's as white as your teeth and your teeth as black as your hair."

He showed us the walls of Ghezel-Hessar, which the prisoners had built and decorated during their forced labour:

"Look, these walls are renewed by your work, every day, but it's your life and your youth that are running away and won't come back. Where's your adored Massoud[3]? Where's your heroic people that's meant

---

3. Massoud Rajavi, historically important leader of the People's Mojahedin.

come and save you? It's true that you won't be allowed to budge from here, but even if you shout as loud as you can, nobody in the world will hear you. This is the end, the end of the world. From here, either you'll go to the cemetery, or you'll learn to be wise. That's what's waiting for you."

With that introduction, I realised that they had brought us here to break us down. We realised later that this was Unit no 1, where were to be found the cage sections, or last judgment sections.

Ping-pong tables forming cages

We'd been waiting for at least four hours. Four hours which seemed like forty. I reviewed the course of events at top speed in my mind, all the girls and the contacts I had with them and the questions that the interrogators could eventually put to me. I prepared my answers. Then I thought of the altercations I'd had during the last few days with the traitresses. I remember having argued with Sharareh who had laughed at the organisation's initials. She had said something insane and I hadn't been able to bear it. I had jumped out of bed and stood in front of her, and said:

"Come on! You can be what you like, a traitress, I don't care a curse! But you'll shut up and not touch the organisation's initials."

I knew she would report it. I was so deeply plunged in my thoughts that when they called Hengameh who was at the head of the queue and we moved forward, I suddenly realised where we were.

Ghezel-Hessar was built over a vast area, and from there they took us in a minibus to Unit no 1. And when I was faced with reality, my fear vanished. They led each of us into a cabin and made us sit down in a corner, with blindfolded eyes.

Each section of Unit no 1 was divided into three, and from what I saw under my bandage when going to the lavatories, there were between forty-eight and fifty-five of us. Hadji Davoud came on the scene and delivered and avalanche of kicks, punches and blows from cables, according to the complaints of his assistant torturers, and repeated in conclusion:

"It's the day of the last judgment, either you come back to the right path, or you go to Hell."

Let's come back to this cage section. This section didn't have the same structure as the others. Each part consisted of wide corridors with a vast room filled with perhaps two hundred ping-pong tables piled up to the ceiling. A year earlier, when we had been transferred from Evin to Ghezel-Hessar, they had brought us at first into a room which was also filled to the ceiling with ping-pong tables. We had joked about it with the girls, laughing:

"Look! They're going to make a games room for us! Nice!"

AT that moment, we were completely ignorant of what their purpose was. But on arriving in the section with cages, I understood what use Lajevardi meant to make of those ping-pong tables. He had meant them to become individual cells which were to break down the Mojahedin prisoners.

In the wide corridor, the tables were set side by side with a gap of at most 70 cm between, and they were linked to one another by soldered iron bars, with a dirty army blanket full of vermin, smelling repulsive, whose threads were like wires that pricked your skin.

In the space between every two tables were the prisoners, crumpled up, their eyes perpetually bandaged. The cages were separated so that nobody could speak to anyone else. Traitresses were on guard night and day over the length and breadth of the place, high and low, to check on the prisoners and make sure they didn't speak to one another.

These cages were so small and narrow that a person of small stature and weighing 50 kg couldn't sit down tailor-fashion, because the sides didn't allow it, and that the board fell on top of the person beside her. Once, to see how it was and to have an idea of the dimensions, I arranged myself slightly tailor-fashion and very gently tried to stretch my leg out a bit. I then felt that one of the board was going to fall. I immediately stopped. The traitress who was watching me said:

"Hypocrite, watch out, you'll break your darling pal's head. But if you want to kill her so as to have more room, say so!"

It was so narrow that even I, who am small, couldn't fit into it. We were obliged all the time to roll ourselves into a ball with our arms round our legs and our heads between our knees so as to manage it.

The first time they took us to make our ablutions and prayers, Hadji Davoud was there. I knew that we had to remain with our eyes bandaged all the time and not move, but I asked Hadji Davoud if I could have a Qur'an or a Nahj-ol-Balagheh[4]. All of a sudden, Hadji's oily laugh rang out:

"You want the Qur'an and the Nahj-ol-Balagheh? Here!"

And he gave me what felt like a bludgeon-stroke on the head.

"And now, what else do you want? Poor hypocrite! Go and think about your misfortune, as if you didn't know where you've landed! eh?"

---

4. A collection of the letters and speeches of Imam Ali, first Shi'ite Imam and son-in-law of the Prophet of Islam.

I laughed at him inwardly, thinking: *poor fool! I'm doing very well where I am. I'd like to make you sweat.*

How to manage perpetual solitude and blackness?

At first, I didn't yet know how long I should stay there, what I should do or how to organise my day. It really was a new world whose rules I didn't know. I didn't yet feel the pain of solitude, the absence of my friends and the lack of that communal life that we had. I could count the days in the week and the hours of the day and night. From morning onwards, I started inside my head to make the programme we had established with the other prisoners, I spoke to them, and I remembered the days we had spent together. Thus I kept up my spirits and stayed happy. I didn't think much about what to do. But after five or six days the pressure of silence began to make itself felt and I couldn't go on remembering. Especially as I had, little by little, reached the conclusion that it wasn't a question of days or even of weeks and I was beginning to take

Hadji's threats seriously: either one cracks and repents, or this situation goes on for a long time, even for years. Then I told myself that I must do something and find a way to fill those endless days and hours.

Alone, my eyes blindfolded and in silence, one becomes a sound-hunter. One seizes the slightest sound, every word, every breath, one analyses it and draws a conclusion from it. One knows when Hadji Davoud comes in. Someone is with him, it's his assistant Ahmad. There, he's speaking to one of those filthy traitresses and she's reporting to him. After a few minutes, we'll hear the blows of a head hitting a wall, perhaps it'll be me! There's the sound of a cooking-pot, it's lunchtime, it's that fat Pasdaran who's bringing it, I recognise him because he drags his feet on the ground.

I think the traitresses who were overseeing us were aware that we were watching for the slightest noise. They murmured among themselves so as to make the prisoners curious and attract their attention to what they were saying. Sometimes, in that way, they used this method to manipulate us. It happened for example that they said, murmuring, but in a manner that was still audible:

"That Azam;s upset because of Mansoureh, whereas she's told everything and she at peace now."

Being crumpled up with blindfolded eyes in silence for hours entails the risk of retreating into oneself and sinking into one's own thoughts and one's imagination. One risks losing one's reason. That was exactly the purpose of those cages. I was as afraid of going mad as of cracking. I told myself that the fatal plans of Khomeini, of the torturer Lajevardi and his pupil Hadji Rahmani must not succeed through me. *No! No! No! Never!* I must prepare myself to endure for a long period. To be on the watch and not to let myself be felled. That's the reason why I made a programme for myself. After waking up and praying, I organised a whole ceremony inside my head. I held myself straight and proudly in front of the organisation's emblem and the Iranian flag, and I began a song. Every day I chose three songs which I sang, then sent greetings: *Long live the prisoners of the resistance who preferred the pain of torture to the shame of betrayal! Greetings! Greetings! Greetings!* I sang three songs that I knew by heart so as not to forget them and not to give in. And when I had forgotten a bit, I repeated the tune so much that I ended up by remembering. When I found passages that I absolutely hadn't remembered before, I was transported with joy and felt I had treasures in my possession.

I had elaborated a programme according to which I knew at what time I had to sing, what I had to sing, and even what I had to think about. I realised that I was beginning to learn to use my brain and how to draw from it the things that were there and that I had forgotten.

Before 20 June 1981, I had a book of songs called *The Mountain* that I had practically learned by heart. But as it was some years since I had hummed them, they had disappeared from my memory. I therefore decided, to occupy my mind, to try to bring back those songs to my memory. My mind got going. To my great astonishment, many things were coming back to me. Every piece that came to the surface was joined to the rest like a puzzle. When I really couldn't remember a passage, I invented something to complete the song. This mental exercise raised my spirits and enabled me to escape.

Then I thought about the books I had read and that I hadn't understood properly or had forgotten. I told myself, for instance: *that subject's one you must find in that history book, or else: remember in which work you read that piece of information.* Or else: *what was that theme linked to? How was the statement constructed?* These reflections enabled me to put my thoughts rigorously in order, to master my mind, and to save me from boredom and sinking into myself. More important still: I discovered the multitude of information – vague and scattered – that my mind contained. Little by little, I learned to remember it, to classify it, to dust it down and to put it back in its proper place. It was as fascinating as the discovery of a new world.

In my programme, thirty minutes were also devoted to the recitation of the Qur'an and the Nahj-ol-Balagheh which I knew by heart. In prison, they were the only works available, with the religious books by those filthy mullahs like Datsgheib, Beheshti, Motahari and co. that they gave us to read. But I only read the Qur'an and the Nahj-ol-Balagheh that I learned by heart and I didn't even glance at the rubbish that the other works represented in my eyes. How glad I was that I had done it! In the section, we came together to learn verses and suras by heart, just like Imam Ali's sermons. Everything I had learned during that period was now my wealth; I drew on it continually in order to preserve the liveliness of my mind. So every day I recited well-known texts, which formed my mental gymnastics. Then I chose a verse and reflected on it.

In the section I came from, we owned a book of religious exegesis called *A Reflection of the Qur'an* written by Father Taleghani[5], that the mothers hid and that we took turns to read. Now that I found myself in the

---

5. Ayatollah Mahmoud Taleghani, a progressive political and religious man who disappeared six months after the revolution. He was extremely popular and close to the People's Mojahedin.

section with the cages in much more terrible conditions than before, what I had learned in that book had become one of my treasures. Sometimes, even the memory of a single sentence that came to the surface enabled me to reflect for a long time.

Among the things I remembered thanks to my mental gymnastics were prayers that I recited with Ashraf Ahmadi who was executed. It happened little by little and they amounted to so much that, when I recited them from beginning to end, it lasted an hour and a half. I was very fond of the prayers of the Ashoura and of Varesse[6], because every sentence traced the enemy's frontiers and that inspired me and taught me how to resist.

When I recited them, I felt I was turning into a rock. Sometimes I thought of my fears when I was first arrested and saw how much I had matured. My universe had changed and my battlefield was now clearly drawn. As if, during that period, I had studied for decades, I had learned to know Khomeini and his fundamentalist ideology. My hatred towards

---

6. A prayer in memory of Imam Hussein.

him had been multiplied by ten and nothing could stop me fighting him.

The more I reflected, the more I understood things that previously had been foreign to me. In particular, the meaning of those verses of the Qur'an that one can only understand on the battlefield. For example there was the verse "ease is found in difficulty" which I had understood to mean "after difficulties comes ease, or in other words, that too will pass, or, as they say, at the end of the night comes the dawn. But, reflecting on it, I told myself: *it doesn't say "after" difficulties but "in" difficulty, in difficulty itself, ease is found! That means that when you think that it's really very difficult and the knife-blade has reached your bones, you put up with it, if you're not afraid and you don't give in. If you make efforts to get out of that difficulty, then doubtless you will reach ease. It's possible on the condition that you don't let yourself be surprised and that you're ready to face any problems.* So one mustn't react to difficulties with sadness, despair and low spirits. "Don't gripe!" Ah! That dear Massoumeh who was recalling herself to me! It was she who had taught me: "A Mojahedin doesn't gripe!" I had experienced it in the cell, during interrogation and under torture.

And then I remembered that when we were taken to be punished, it was our daily lot. The torturers had thrown us into that section and every day they increased the pressure to break us down and make us give in. But, faced with the enemy, we gained strength and were full of energy; we had then passed from "burden" to "ease". Now that I found myself in this cage, in these conditions created to crush us, if I resisted, if I managed to reduce the torturer's efforts to nothing, if, faced with the ordeals sowed throughout my fight, I remained patient and firm, I would reach "ease". That was how I made myself discover and learn the laws of this new world.

The law of absolute silence

In the cage, there was a law of complete silence. We had absolutely no rright to speak. In case of need, we had to raise a hand and keep it in the air for as long as it took for the Pasdaran or the traitress to see it and choose the moment to come to us. And then the person approached and pressed their wretched mouth to the prisoner's ear to say:

"Speak softly!"

If we spoke the slightest bit too loudly, blows rained down and the guards reported that we had tried to communicate with another prisoner. In that case, it was Hadji Davoud and Ahmad who came over to beat us violently on the head. They hit the prisoner's face and head against the wall with the aim, as they admitted loud and clear, of bringing her to death's door in order to cure her of the slightest wish to ask for anything.

Before a meal was distributed, the guards gave me a blow on the head. That meant "eat". However, most of the time, I was deprived of meals. Their motions and the sound of dishes made me understand that they were distributing a meal. When it was over, they asked: "Who hasn't had a meal?" to see who would raise her hand. And as I didn't raise my hand, it often happened that I didn't eat. They said to me:

"Hypocrite! You'll end up by needing us one day."

I refused to bend.

As a result of under-nourishment and hunger, towards the last days, I had become so weak that, when they came to look for me to go to prayers and pulled on my chador to make me stand up, I couldn't stay on my legs, which were stiff after staying too long in the same position. They therefore pulled me up by force. When I stood up, I fell to the ground, flat on my face like a rag doll. They traitors and the Pasdaran mocked me, laughing:

"The heroine's fallen!"

Hadji Davoud, the torturer, went on with a ringing, oily laugh:

"We'll keep you here till you die. I'll make you hope to leave here with the title of tortured Mojahedin. I shan't let you become a heroine! I'm the champion, I'm the one who'll make the hypocrites bend."

One day, many months earlier, Ali Khamenei's brother[7] had come, escorted by a

---

7. Ali Khamenei was President of Khomeini's republic. After the latter's

delegation, into our section, No 7. Mrs Efat Shabestari, a mother of a family aged 65, was among us. Arthrosis gnawed all her joints and she didn't have the strength to walk. That's why she had remained at the end of the section without going out. One of Khamenei's brother's escorts who, it appears, was related to that lady, had said to her ironically:

"You who are so brave, come here and have a talk!"

And he had obliged her to leave her cell to come to the section entrance. Because of arthrosis and the total lack of medicaments, she walked with difficulty and had finally fallen down. The delegation that had supposedly come to hear the prisoners' complaints had started to laugh and mock her.

"You who used to be so strong, how come you can't even manage to walk?"

In spite of the seriousness of her condition, she had a steely spirit. And there in my heart I had answered in her stead: *Laugh, you imbeciles! Yes, I'm falling and I'll fall again, but I'll never bend. I'm the one who'll end by*

---

death, he became the regime's Supreme Leader.

winning. You are destined for defeat.

Thenceforward, while I was living in the cage unit, when I fell down myself and the torturers laughed, I remembered all the scenes and all the words of those days and silently repeated: *Yes, I'm falling, but I don't bend. We'll see who will end up losing and who'll be the winner!*

Blows, always blows

For seven days, day and night, all our basic rights were denied us. All day, without moving, without making the slightest sound, a blindfold over our eyes, sitting in the fetal position. We couldn't even lean against the sides of the cage. If we leaned on them, the sides fell on the head of the prisoner next to us and blows rained down. During the day, we couldn't sleep or doze. The slightest sign of dozing, just like the slightest sound, even the act of coughing or sneezing without meaning to was considered a wish to give a signal to the others and earned us a rain of blows. Always blows.

At midnight, they gave us the order to

sleep. The cage was so short that in spite of being 1.57 m, I didn't fit into it completely. And when I wanted to put my head on the ground, I fell on the bar that soldered the two beds together and whose sharpened edge cut into my flesh. When they gave us permission to sleep, we had to do it in the same clothes, the same chador and the same blindfold over our eyes. But that was the moment when the blows from cables arrived. Because from midnight onwards, Hadji Davoud and his torturer Ahmad came, cable in hand, to the cage section to give us our ration of blows.

From midnight onwards, they put the radio full on to stop us sleeping. They did that every evening. At first it was unbearable to me as what with tiredness and the pressures of the day, I wanted to have at least a little peace and sleep for a few hours. But I had to transform all that the enemy used to break us down into a positive element for myself. I saw that it was an excellent opportunity to collect and store documents on which I could reflect during the day. For example, every day they transmitted the sermon from a town's

Friday prayers, which enabled me to keep up to date with current events. Especially on Friday, when they transmitted the grand prayer from Tehran, I gathered an enormous lot of information. I was very satisfied with the new means I had found, I was no longer sleepy, my mind was lively and I searched to find what I could draw from every broadcast that passed.

I learned an enormous lot: from verses of the Qur'an or the Nahj-ol-Balagheh that they sometimes transmitted, to the poems that they recited during the "Path of Night" broadcast, from the imams' Friday sermons to the "Work and Worker" broadcast that reflected the people's misery. Or topics concerning drugs and other broadcasts. Some programmes were really ridiculous and I laughed, all stretched out. Sometimes too, during the "Work and Worker" broadcast that they transmitted at 6 in the morning, one heard news of the labourers' and workers' situation that reflected, in spite of censorship, their sad situation. For me it was a good source of reflection and that motivated my resistance.

I had learned to sleep during the day, sitting up, without the Pasdaran and the traitresses seeing it, and that's how I compensated for the sleepless nights without getting caught.

The meals weren't given at fixed times. It was according to their own sweet will. The same applied to prayers or going to the lavatories. In theory, they took us to the lavatories three times a day but sometimes not at all. And when they took us to the lavatories, they didn't leave us even a minute. As soon as we went in, to harass us, they opened the door immediately, saying;

"Hypocrite, it's over!"

Because of the pressures and the stress, I had fallen ill and I couldn't do anything in a minute. That's how I had convulsions. The pain all over my body, caused by the long hours spent sitting rolled in a ball, was such that I could no longer stand on my feet. Especially as that sitting position had hurt my feet. Sometimes I used my legs as a chair, so as to hurt less, but I could only bear it for a few minutes.

If I moved a little to change my position, those torturers hit me on the head, shouting:

"Hypocrite, what's eating you? Why are you moving so much? Are you itching?"

Then they made a report, and in the evening there was a fresh rain of blows falling on my head. Pains added to other pains.

A lesson and some modelling in the cage

One of my activities in the cage was teaching. I reminded myself, going over them mentally, of the courses I had taught and each of the little children I loved so much, with their name and their place in class. I taught them what I had learned, with their own words. Sometimes memories came back, I thought of their problems and wept. Sometimes I thought of their questions and their hopes. I said to them in my mind: *My children, I haven't forgotten you. My darlings, you will soon recover the feeling of tenderness, pleasure and tranquillity and you will see Iran happy and prosperous.*

I remembered little Mansoureh, so sweet

and pleasant, who came to school in the depths of winter with just a pinafore. Her red cheeks burning with cold, in tears, she pressed herself against the heater to warm herself. As to Fatemeh, she always hid under the table to cry because, during a quarrel between her parents, she had hidden behind the bed. She had heard her father say that he couldn't feed them any longer and that he was going to put the children in the orphanage and her mother had threatened to douse herself with petrol and burn herself if he dared to do that. And that kid dreaded to find her mother dead when she came home.

I comforted them in my imagination and told them that when the revolution came, Mansoureh's father would find a good job and could buy her a coat, good shoes and warm clothes. Fatemeh's father would have a good salary and wouldn't send them to the orphanage. I said to Fatemeh's mother: *Why burn yourself? Stay patient for a while longer, everything will work out all right. The children will grow, they'll go to school and university and find a good job and you too will be happy.*

I thought again about my friend Roghieh Akbari's little daughter: one day, at Ghezel-Hessar Prison, I had noticed that Roghieh's mind was elsewhere. I asked her:

"What are you thinking about? Tell me so that I can do it too, even from a distance."

I had learned that phrase in a poem in the *Mojahed* newspaper in 1980. It was written beside Mohammad Reza Saadati's photo[8]. Roghieh had lifted her head:

"I don't know why, suddenly I thought of my daughter Mahnaz and in my heart I was praying God that my daughter should become a Mojahedin."

"How old is she?"

"She's only little, but what is important is that she's my daughter and I feel that she's sure to become a Mojahedin."

I drew strength from those people and said to myself: *it's for them that you are in a cage. If you want the Mansourehs and Fatemehs to be always unhappy and without a future,*

---

8. A political prisoner in the Shah's time, Mohammad Reza Saadati was arrested again a few months after the Revolution by Khomeini's regime on the pretext that he was spying. He was actually taken hostage to put pressure on the PMOI. Following a scandalous judgment, he was condemned to ten years in prison, but was executed in 1981.

get up and be like those sham revolutionaries who didn't last a week. Go to the torturers and repent. Go and tell them that you've converted to Hadji's Islam and that you've only just understood how wrong you were. But you're a Mojahedin! You know that in this world you must give an account of yourself and you know why you're here. So you must bear it and you can bear it. I said to that gorilla Hadji: We know which of us will end by winning.

During my time in the cage, I spent part of my time planning a Persian book for the children of CE2. What texts I should put in, and in each lesson and each text, what points I must emphasise. Every day, in my mind, I completed it. After a time, I had mentally organised the best part of the book. That's how I occupied myself and sometimes I really didn't notice time passing or the day going on. In the evening, before going to sleep, I thought at first of what I was going to do next day. At first I expected to do the same as the previous day. But immediately I realised that I mustn't reason in that way, that I mustn't repeat myself, that this was what was wearing. It would have shut me into myself and the enemy would have won. And then I told myself that, a few minutes later, they would put on the radio, I must listen very attentively to see what was new so that I could use it in the next day's programme, so that my daily programme shouldn't be tiring or repetitive. That enabled me to feel the lack of sleep and get rid of the pressure. My mind grew active and I searched all the time for new subjects for reflection.

Sometimes, I gave myself intelligence tests or played games like the baccalaureate to entertain myself. For example, I chose the letter B and looked for names, town, countries, personalities, fruits beginning with B. It was a good intellectual exercise and a pastime. And that wasn't as tiring as thinking. Especially as that game which dated from my childhood enabled me to remember that time. I remembered my friends from those days, the girls from the cell with whom I had played that game too and I thought about them.

Days in the cage resembled one another

and went by in silence. Sometimes an incident broke the routine. Once, after perhaps three days without meals, a Pasdaran gave me a plate of food and a piece of bread, accompanied by a blow on the head. Now at the sight of the meal, my stomach turned over. I could no longer eat. That day I wasn't feeling well and I had the blues. I put the plate on the ground. I thought about my fellow-prisoners. I remembered "Kheyrieh Safa'i" with whom I had spent a few days in Section 4 of Ghezel-Hessar. Kheyrieh was executed a few years later during the great slaughter of Mojahedin political prisoners in 1988[9]. As speaking to one another was forbidden in Section 4, she

9. In August 1988, Khomeini decided to carry out his final solution to liquidate almost all the political prisoners. With a terrible fatwa, in a few months he set in motion carnage unprecedented in contemporary Iranian history. He ordered the swiftest possible execution of those who persisted in their convictions in favour of the People's Mojahedin. Death squads, for whom those responsible still remain in their jobs in Iran, carried out Khomeini's order to slaughter by hanging over 30,000 political prisoners of whom an enormous majority belonged to the PMOI. Some were killed with grenades in the cells. Most had been incarcerated for several years. Many had served their sentences. Men, women and children were hastily buried in communal graves, notably at Khavaran in South Tehran. Ayatollah Monazeri, Khomeini's heir at the time, had protested against "the execution of several thousand people in a few days". Which earned him dismissal and being placed under forced residence. Amnesty International described this slaughter as a crime against humanity and demanded that those responsible be brought to justice.

communicated with me by means of gestures and looks which I answered with smiles. One day, I sat down beside her and asked:

"But why do you take so many precautions? Since I've been there, you've only spoken to me with signs and looks!"

"Every time I speak to someone, they take her away and throw her in the punishment cell and hit her," she answered with tears in her eyes. If only they'd take me and hit me instead."

While we were speaking, she had made a figurine with breadcrumbs. A little girl.

"Look, it's a figurine of one of my best friends who died a martyr. I'll offer it to you."

Remembering Kheyrieh, I felt better. In her memory, I put some bread in the stew and when it was slightly impregnated with sauce I took it. I was softening it when all of a sudden a guard arrived and, hitting me on the head, told me to give him the plate. I gave him the plate with one hand and he didn't see the crumbs I had kept in the other. When he had gone, I went on softening them. I had decided to make a figurine of them. I had never made any, I don't know why I wanted so much to do it. In my childhood, I'd been told that a woman, to have a confidante, had made a wax doll and called it "Syngue Sabour" (patience stone [10] and confided all her troubles to it. It's perhaps the need to speak to someone that had pushed me into making a figurine. I remembered my martyred friends, Hadjar, Mahdokht, Simine, Atieh and I decided to make a figurine of them in effigy so as to speak to them. I started to make one, looking from underneath my blindfold and my chador. I no longer remember who it was and I began to speak to her. I was immersed in this work when, all of a sudden, I was slapped on the back and told to get up. I was frightened and thought that the guard had noticed the figurine. If he had seen it and caught it, I should certainly have had a ton of blows. I hid it at top speed in my pocket and stood up. But it was time for the lavatories and for prayer. I was so deeply immersed in that

10. In Persian mythology, this is a magic stone that one puts in front of one-self to unleash on it one's troubles, one's suffering, one's pains, one's miseries … One confides to it everything one wouldn't dare reveal to others. And the stone listens, absorbs all words and all secrets like a sponge until one fine day it bursts. That's the day when one is set free.

work that I hadn't noticed the time passing. I was happy and, when I came back, I went on. With the crumbs I had left, I made some other figurines, and spoke to them for hours. Thanks to those little breadcrumb dolls, my heart was lighter and my spirits rose again. I no longer felt ill or tired.

Another time, going to the lavatories, I saw a little comb and on it, with a pin, someone had carved "Your friend Shouri." I understood that my dear Shouri had left it there for me on purpose. The guards hadn't noticed. I hid it in my clothes so as to bring it back. I had a hair-slide and when I sat down, I took it off my head. With the pin I had, I began to write, and I managed to finish before going back to the lavatories. "Received. All of you whose number I don't know, I love you. Azam Hadj." I put down the comb exactly where I'd found it. When I wanted to go out, the guard came back like a fury. I was frightened because I thought it was she who had put the comb there to test me. No! the guard had left me there longer than usual and she wanted to bark for a few moments to retrieve her mistake. The next time, I saw that there hair-slide was no longer there. I was very happy to have been able to make contact with one of the girls of whom I was very fond. For a whole hour, I cudgelled my brains to find out what I could leave and how I could make contact with Hengameh and the other girls I knew were here.

On 28 June 1984, on the anniversary of the death of Beheshti[11] and his entourage, the Pasdaran and the interrogators stuck their faces and heads like madmen and uttered howls. They came to check on us and started their goings-on again. Their howls were so ridiculous that I began to laugh. One of them, who was behind me, understood that I was laughing and let Hadji Davoud know. The latter kicked me so hard in the back that my head struck the wall. It made such a noise that I thought I had broken my teeth. With my hand, I checked that they were in place. Hadji Davoud was hitting me savagely and wouldn't stop repeating:

"You're not getting hit enough! Shedding

---

11. The second in command of the regime and chief of judiciary power.

hypocrites' blood is allowed and you've been alive too long. You're the assassin of Beheshti and his friends and the imam said that we can shed your blood and plunder your goods and you oughtn't to be breathing!"

He was hitting to kill.

Because of my sitting down too long, my back and all my limbs were hurting. Every blow cut off my breath. I felt my bones breaking and told myself that nothing would be left of me. It was only because of my intention to resist the torturers that I endured the pressures and the hunger. But, on a physical level, I was half paralysed. I had the feeling that my bones were hollow; sometimes I couldn't move my hand and I needed to use the other hand to manage it. Sometimes I was like a totally dry statue, unable to make the slightest gesture, as if my body no longer belonged to me. That's why every kick from Hadji propelled me here and there like a ball. Especially as my eyes were blindfolded; consequently, I could see nothing and couldn't control my movements. It was incredible but, in spite of the very sharp pain and my state of complete physical weakness, in my heart I rejoiced and felt triumphant. I told him: *Hit me, we'll see who will be broken in the end and who will win. You or me? It's certain, I'm the one who'll win, because I am a Mojahedin.* I had forgotten the pain. That day, Hadji Davoud wouldn't stop coming back to hit me, without being able to break me down. But I wasn't the only one being struck; he was hitting the others like a madman as well. Seeing the girls being so savagely beaten made me suffer. I don't know who was beaten but, hearing the screams, the noises and the comings and goings of the agents, I understood that I wasn't the only one.

After all those blows, that evening I wanted one thing only: to sleep. I was worn out but the terrible noise of the radio after midnight didn't give us a moment's rest. And on top of that, there was the nightmare of the presence of Hadji Davoud who kept coming back to hit us for one reason or another. It was he who had called this section "the last judgment", where we had to give an account of ourselves. He said that if we had a tranquil moment, we should start thinking of resistance. Poor imbecile! He didn't know that it was his actions that made us think most of resistance because it proved that our struggle was well-founded. Those who could doubt that, here in prison, saw their doubts turning into convictions and they shouted as hard as they could: "Long live the Mojahedin! Long live Massoud, who from the first day knew how to unmask that bloodthirsty Khomeini and all his troop."

That time, even if I was KO, I rejoiced at the sight of the torturer in that state. One day, I was in Jomhouri Street and I spent four hours getting out of that quarter. That day, wherever I went, I saw that the Pasdaran had attacked. They had started raids on the homes of everyone I knew. I took a taxi to get away from the district. A Pasdaran began to hit the bonnet like a madman, telling the driver that he mustn't work because Beheshti had been killed. But the taxi-driver answered: if he didn't work, how would he feed his family? We were afraid that the driver would awake his suspicions of my friend and me and that we would be arrested.

"Come on, calm yourself! We've other things to do!" I said to the driver.

"It's not a criminal who's gone to Hell who'll stop me working, my little lady!"

"Listen, we're Mojahedin, please take us where we need to go as fast as you can."

The driver showed himself very pleased to hear it.

"So that you can reach your destination as fast as possible, I'll calm myself and I shan't answer them!"

We all looked at each other, smiling.

The blows, that day, made me go over my memories, easing my pain. Every day I had a subject about which to think. The prisoners who found themselves detained in those conditions were physically destroyed but, morally, they found reasons every day to motivate themselves.

A bruised body

Imagine sitting crouched down, unable to move, on your heels, not for a day or two, or even a week or two, but for seven long months! With poor feeding and often no food, my physical state began to show signs of progressive deterioration. My muscles were stiff, they seemed made of wood, and I hurt all over. It was as if my body was covered with wounds. When punches and kicks rained on me, especially during the last few weeks, I thought my muscles and my bones would break at any moment. I felt extreme heat all over my body, particularly on the soles of my feet. So when I could, taking care not to attract the torturers' attention, I pulled the rough blanket from under my feet to relieve myself by putting them on the cold stones of the floor. That feverish heat stifled me. The stomach pains caused by hunger were so sharp that they made me desperate. But I told myself at once that I must resist by ignoring them. I sometimes felt I had lost all my strength. My dried-out intestines tormented me because I hadn't eaten my fill for a long time. Only blood came out when I went to the lavatories where I often wept, I was suffering so much. At least, in the lavatories, I was alone and those tears relieved me a little. I tried to seem calm and serene when I came out because they must not notice how much I was hurting: if they detected a weak point, they would exploit it to the full to break me or, at least, they would rejoice and feel triumphant at having inflicted such suffering on me. When I cried, I felt ashamed and said to myself: *Azam! You're crying? You? No, never, never! No, you've never been weak! Have you already forgotten your friends' courage and endurance under the most atrocious tortures?* Then I remembered them, one after another ... Simine Hojabr, Doctor Hadjar Robat-Karami, Fatemeh Assef, Sima Sharifpour, Doctor Mahdokht Mohammadi-Zadeh ... *Don't you belong to the Mojahedin generation? So why are you crying from pain?* The torturers, overflowing with hatred and exasperated, shouted at me:

"We'll end up by breaking you, you slip of a girl! You're hurting no one but yourself!"

And I answered them in my heart: *Come and fight and we'll see!* Over twenty years later, the physical results of those seven and a half months are clearly visible. Chronic digestive illnesses, painful bone diseases, traumatisms of the joints and neurological problems ... I lost most of my teeth in prison. Because of a general gum infection, about ten of my teeth were pulled out in one month. Practically toothless from 1981 to 1986, I was obliged to do half my chewing with my gums, which progressively damaged them. Even today, in spite of all their efforts, the dentists of Ashraf haven't been able to remake my teeth satisfactorily.

During the last days spent in that cage, I had lost my memory to the point of forgetting most of what I knew by heart, even the prayers that I said several times a day. Even the thought of losing my reason terrified me. *Have I gone mad?* Sometimes I complained to God, sobbing, although I had pledged not to: *but where is Thy mercy, Lord?*

A bestial weapon for breaking women

One day when pain was drowning me, I was taken to the guards' room and forced to stay standing for half a day. Then Hadji Davoud came and shouted at me:

"Come on, we'll talk. You defend your ideas and I'll defend the imam, we'll see which of us will convince the other."

Almost as soon as he had finished his sentence, I fell to the ground, being unable to stand any longer. Some torturers and interrogators who were questioning prisoners came towards me:

"You see how you're dying, you wretch? You can't even manage to stand up. How do you expect to resist or struggle? Who are you struggling for? Who do you want to die for? Think of yourself and your family for a bit! Look what you've done to yourself!"

While that torturer was shouting his "advice" at me, I watched our martyrs, my companions in the struggle, filing past: from the founders of the organisation, Mohammad Hanifnejad, Saïd Mohsen and Ali-Asghar Badizadegan, through Fatemeh Amini[12], Mehdi Rezaï[13] and the epic of their

---

12. The first woman member of the PMOI killed under torture by the Savak, the Shah's political police.

13. The Rezaï family lost eight of their children in the resistance to the dictatorship of the Shah, then to that of Khomeini. Mehdi Rezaï was the third son executed by one of the Shah's military courts. At 19 years old he became a symbol for Iranian youth.

resistance and their deaths. I could only bow humbly before their memory. Thinking of them, I recovered some strength, I rose and held on firmly to the wall so as not to fall again. Noticing my gesture, Hadji Davoud, very angrily, shouted to his men:

"Leave her! Leave her standing so that she'll die! But in fact, she's a nice girl, don't bother her too much!"

It was like a coded message among them. From then on, every time a torturer came up to me to assault me sexually, he would say to me:

"But you're still the same nice girl!"

Powerless, no longer able to react as before to those ignoble acts, I was often seized with convulsions. As they didn't manage to make a Mojahedin woman break down, they had recourse to that bestial weapon.

At times, when I underwent those ordeals, I wept, but a few moments later, I said to myself: *Don't forget that they're doing all that to break you down ... It's like lashes, what's the difference?* That's what enabled me to hold on.

For a long time, as if it had been my turn to be lashed, they came and pulled me by my chador, dragged me out of the room, without saying a word for fear of alerting the other prisoners in the cage section, and inflicted sexual assaults on me right behind the door. After spending several months, night and day, in the cage without letting anyone hear me cry under that pressure and those intolerable pains, those bestial acts weakened me.

It was nightmarish to hear the sound of someone approaching: *Who is it? What does he want to do to me?* One day I decided to attack with all my strength the first man who came up to me with that aim. I concentrated as hard as I could to hear the man who tried to approach. In spite of the blindfold over my eyes, I was able to glimpse a man arriving. Then I gave him the strongest kick I could. My reaction took him by surprise, especially as he had seen me fall a short while before. Then he gave me two or three kicks before going away and I was taken back to my cage. I was at once full of joy and filled with shame at not having done the same thing sooner. Once again I had learned a lesson: the torturer draws back when a prisoner takes the offensive.

The next morning, I was taken to the shower. Every time they took a prisoner to the shower, they checked that there was no trace left of the prisoner before, because if we knew of the presence of one of ourselves, especially if we found out who it was, it became a source of hope and resistance. The gaolers wanted to make us believe that all the others had given up, that they had left, and that we were the only ones continuing to undergo those ordeals. That day, going into the shower room, I didn't have the strength to wash myself at all, but I saw a clothes line with clothes drying. I was able to see friends' names on the blouses. I also noticed a soap dish with "Shouri" written on it and a washing glove in another corner with another girl's name. I was so happy; it was as if I had seen them in person. I was mad with joy, to the point of bursting out laughing. Even if there were only five minutes left of the ten which I had for showering, I felt so light that I showered and washed my clothes in five minutes. I was ready when the mercenaries came to bring me back to the quarter. My eyes remained fixed on the clothes and I took pleasure in seeing the women guards fidgeting and getting irritable. My behaviour showed them how stupid and clumsy they were. A guard took hold of my chador and pulled me towards her, shouting insults and howling:

"I don't know why we take you to the showers you …!"

But I was happy and said to myself: *Bravo Azam! You've scored a point!*

In that war of attrition, I had set myself the goal of achieving a victory or gaining something every day. In spite of all my suffering, that feeling of victory was very pleasant.

Another of the torturers' methods of breaking us down consisted in pretending to talk among themselves about the prisoners whom they knew to be our very close friends. They would say, for example:

"You see? So and so has finally given up and gone away to get her life back … while that one's rotting here for nothing."

Later on, after having been released, the girls who were in the same section as I was told how the traitress nicknamed *Gestapo* walked about murmuring to her companions, so as to be heard by everyone, the names of some prisoners in the cage – Azam, Shouri, Hengameh – who had supposedly consented to "give interviews". She tried in this way to undermine the prisoners' spirits.

On their side, to show that they were still there, our friends tried to make a noise by sneezing, coughing or heaving a sigh when they went to the lavatories or passed near the cages. Naturally, they were all conscious of the price they would have to pay in terms of violence, but they were ready to do it in order to stay in touch.

One evening, the gaolers called six prisoners. I was among them. They made us walk towards another section where there was a wall and thick iron bars. I remember especially a girl I was very fond of Sepideh Zargar, a nurse with twelve years of professional experience. She had almost totally lost her eyesight because of the blows on the head she had been given and could no longer see without glasses. The gaolers often deprived her of her glasses to put even more pressure on her. Sepideh was finally executed for refusing to participate in a televised interview expressing repentance.

That evening, we stood up for several hours in a nearby corridor. After one or two hours, I felt dizzy. Feeling unable to stay upright, I said so to a Pasdaran who retorted:

"You hypocrite, you're cheating!"

He had hardly finished insulting me when I fainted and as I fell I knocked a friend who fell down as well. I didn't realise I had fallen until my head hit the ground. Seeing me on the floor, one Pasdaran said to the other;

"See if she's still breathing."

They were visibly embarrassed and said to each other:

"Those hypocrites are doing everything in order to accuse us of having killed them!"

In the cage section, hygiene was catastrophic. We were deprived of minimal living conditions. For example, the prisoners were allowed to take a shower every twenty days, and we had only ten minutes to do it and wash our clothes. Seizing every opportunity to humiliate us, once they gave me a plastic bucket filled with dirty water from washing the floor. The Pasdaran woman howled:

"Here! Hypocrite! That's the shit from your feet! Go on, empty it and use it!"

But as I couldn't bear that disgusting water, I washed my clothes at the same time as I showered. I had to leave at the end of the "compulsory" ten minutes, otherwise they opened the door, howling:

"Get out of there, otherwise we'll get you out by force!"

Sometimes, the gaolers dragged us out on the pretext of a fresh interrogation, forced us to go round the section or another one, to get into cars, in order to terrify us even more by creating the atmosphere of an execution. They shouted at us:

"Make your minds up! Either you go back to being normal or we'll relieve you from this life of suffering!"

To keep the prisoners constantly in the fear and anguish of another interrogation, they also took us to the guards' room and made us wait, standing up, for hours. Another method consisted in playing a tape of people howling under torture. In short, they had to keep each prisoner in a constant state of terror, fear and anguish in order to make her yield or break her down and force her to repent.

FIFTH PART

The result of the war

Victory!

The horror of the cage section had lasted over seven months when one day some men sent by Montazeri[1] arrived and were able to speak to one or two prisoners.

"Tell us, what's happening here?" they asked one of them.

"With our eyes blindfolded, how can I see what's happening? Your eyes aren't blindfolded, so look for yourselves!"

Then that mullah came towards me

---

1. Ayatollah Hossein-Ali Montazeri was at first Khomeini's heir. But that highest Shi'ite dignitary opposed the massacre of political prisoners in 1988, which led to his dismissal and being placed under forced residence. He died at the end of 2009 after having opposed the Supreme Leader, regretting that he had at one time guaranteed the principle of the Velayat-e-Faghih (supremacy of the religious leader).

saying:

"Don't blame Islam for those things; we've come to examine the situation!"

The torturer Lajevardi had just been replaced. As he had failed, it seemed to us that the regime wanted to show that things had changed. However, in spite of his departure, Lajevardi went on working in his office on the third floor of the "revolutionary" Prosecution Service; and those who passed through that building had seen him many times.

That day, those men spoke of a heap of things before filming everything and then leaving.

Three days later, while we were still there, they picked up the wooden boards and took the blindfolds off our eyes. At last we were able to see each other again. When my blindfold was taken off, I saw Shouri first. She was smiling, as always. Then I saw Hengameh with that spark in her eyes and she too had a smile on her lips. It was incredible! It was the most beautiful vision that I could be offered after seven months spent with my eyes blindfolded. I was the happiest woman in the world. I smiled in my turn. Farther off, I glimpsed my dear Sepideh who was looking fixedly at us, as if she were saying to us with her look: *you see, we've won at last!*

While I was watching this magical scene in silence, I felt tears of joy rolling down my cheeks. When the mercenaries left, leaving us alone, Shouri came to kiss me.

"Why are you crying?"

I put my head on her shoulder and cried for some long minutes. She stroked my hair gently:

"You see? It's over!"

"I've forgotten everything, dear Shouri. I'm going daft!"

She took my head between her hands and looked me in the eyes. I'll never forget how gentle her face was or the spark in her eyes, sign of an unshakeable will and determination.

"Azam, you're crying? There's nothing serious!"

Shouri was a doctor. I spoke to her of my health. She listened to me calmly and patiently and then she told me that all that was because of malnutrition and that I should soon get all my strength back and my memory too …

"Shouri," I said to her, reassured, "I'm withdrawing the share of my tears that I shed for myself, but I'm asking you to accept these tears of joy that I've shed on finding you again."

She burst out laughing. On the other side of the room, Hengameh was confiding in me with her revealing looks. It was as if each one was communicating to the others what had happened during those long months. We could have summed up all that history in a few words: "Fighting to stay human."

I got up and looked more attentively at the others. Each one gave a cry of joy and astonishment at finding a very close friend:

"Oh God! But what's happened to you?"

It's true that in the course of less than a year, we had all aged fifteen or twenty years. Lacking mirrors, no one could see her own face, but the sight of the others' faces filled us with sadness. We naturally hadn't imagined we had undergone the same physical deterioration.

Finding each of my friends enabled me to get my strength back. Being unable to sit down, I walked up and down the room. Hengameh was talking loudly, in a lively and joyous voice; she was telling jokes and imitating Hadji, laughing. Fearing the sneaks who might cause her trouble, I called to her:

"A bit of calm, little one, let's see where we are first!"

"Ah, leave me alone! What more can that Hadji do to us? What more can they do than they've already done?" she retorted with the same defiant spirit that was characteristic of her.

She went on with her games and jokes.

Seeing all those friends again, I got my memory back, as if the parts of my body were being filled with an elixir of life. Remembering that we had overcome the enemy in spite of all his bestiality, my heart beat joyfully and I had a great feeling of pride in finding myself beside those heroines.

They were laughing with tears in their eyes. I could read their looks and hear them shouting, as I had inside my head: *Lajevardi!*

You've seen how your plan and your inhuman theory have fallen down? You've seen how we've made you bite the dust? And to Hadji Rahmani: *You cowardly imbecile! Why are you hiding? Where's your bragging gone? Come and see who's won! Come and see who the heroes are!*

I was in a hurry to go back to the section to see the girls again. We knew from the loudspeakers what the torturers said, speaking of the cages: "It's a place like the last judgment or Hell …" So I wanted most urgently to go back to the section to tell them of the failure of that "last judgment" project. I missed them all. I had so many things to tell them. And they had, too! Certainly a lot of things had happened in the section …

So that Hell that had only been, in fact, a merciless battle between Khomeini and the Mohjahedin had ended in our victory and the enemy's total defeat.

The inhuman enemy had created that section because he thought that all the Mojahedin prisoners would crack at the end of a week or a month at most, that they would give in and repent. Having obtained no results in spite of all his executions, he thought that his problem arose from the fact that he didn't have enough space available for isolation cells and that, put in solitary confinement, the prisoners would change their ground one by one at the end of a month. That's the reason why they had created the Hell of cages and coffins whose conditions were much more appalling than those of solitary confinement in cells. But at the end of it all, they had been obliged to stand the blow, admit their defeat and get rid of Lajevardi, although only provisionally, to try to defuse the severe criticism that that torturer's tactics had produced. They only knew ignoble beings like themselves and not real human beings determined to resist.

Quarantine

Having dismantled the cage quarter, the torturers realised that they couldn't immediately transfer the prisoners who had come out of the cages to the ordinary quarters. For after seven months spent crouched down, with blindfolded eyes, in those infernal conditions, none of us was in a normal physical state. We were therefore living proof of the regime's barbarity and bestiality.

If they let us into the communal quarters, even if they deprived us of visits from our families, it was certain that the other prisoners would send out information during visits, and that this information would circulate. So it was decided to keep us in the same place for two months in what they themselves called a sort of quarantine so that we could recover our human appearance. For example, our eyes had lost their natural state, especially as we had often tried to see in spite of the blindfold. Besides, we were too weak to stand or walk.

All the same, rumours of the existence of the cages had circulated and the families who had no news of their children for months were insisting that the authorities should allow visits to them. Consequently, the regime had given in to the pressure and granted, after a month's hesitation, family visits to some prisoners. The parents were so shocked by their children's physical state that they tried to find out the reason for it.

Personally, I remained almost completely deprived of visits during the five and a half years that I spent in prison. After her liberation at the end of two years' captivity, my elder sister Mahine went regularly, for years, to the prisons at Evin and Ghezel-Hessar. She waited for hours behind the door in the hope of gaining permission to see us, me or our younger sister Najmeh, who had given birth to one of her two children behind the bars. Not only did the guards refuse to allow a single visit, but they even refused to answer simple questions like the name of the prison where we were being detained or if we were still alive. For many years, Mahine tried to see us while carrying in her arms Najmeh's disabled child, who was paralysed. As well as their refusal to allow visits, the Pasdaran threatened and intimidated her. Finally, at the end of the caging and because public opinion had been informed of it, she gained the right to one or two visits to Najmeh and myself. But they stopped all visits shortly afterwards.

The survivors of the residential quarter

A few prisoners who had been sent to the residential quarter had been brought back to quarantine. In that section, the Pasdaran and the torturers were allowed to commit all the odious acts that they wished on the prisoners. The Pasdaran called that section "the Harem" among themselves. The prisoners were regarded as prey and slaves.

Most of them had lost their mental balance because of the physical and psychological pressured they had undergone. The case of Shiva, a technology student, was particularly serious. Very intelligent, talented, lively-minded and creative, she had become mentally ill in the residential quarter. She was afraid of the group and very quickly isolated herself.

She had a cardboard box in which she had put a tray, a spoon, a glass, a Qur'an, a prayer book and a little prayer mat. She put it in front of her and propped herself up on a pillow and a blanket. In that way, she had created an exclusive "zone" about 70 cm wide and forbade anyone to come near it. Once, in the lavatories, while I was washing my hands, I splashed her without meaning to. She started to hit her head with both hands for about ten to fifteen minutes and then fainted! For half an hour, nobody dared go near her, for fear of setting her off again.

As to Farzaneh, she always wore a long red dress, and walked about the quarter talking to herself, saying senseless things, before bursting into laughter or tears. She spent hours sitting in a corner, staring at her bag. Sometimes, she went up to the others who were asleep and looked at them as if she was going to strangle them at any minute. From time to time, she went to the showers or the lavatories and made indescribably disgusting and pathetic scenes.

Thus the residential quarter, much more frightening than the cage one, had caused irreversible mental illness among some of the prisoners.

After two months spent in quarantine, we had more or less recovered a human appearance. That's why they were able to bring us back to Section 8 where we stayed about a month.

In that Section 8, the guards had agreed on establishing the following programme: the traitresses' mission consisted in provoking brawls and quarrels, so as to put a bit more pressure on the prisoners. But they didn't have much success because stories of the cages had circulated in the prisoners' families, even reaching some levels of the outside world, provoking a particular "social impact". The torturers rechristened Section 8 the "liberty" quarter! They transferred prisoners at the end of their sentences there and also another group that they claimed to have pardoned. The prisoners who had come out of the cages were transferred to Sections 3 and 4. I was transferred to 4. They wanted to give Section 8 a "normal" appearance. Nonetheless, they continued to keep that quarter under strict surveillance, employing fresh groups of Pasdaran and other mercenaries there to keep a closer watch on the situation, all obviously in order to display the spectacle of a "free space".

They said, for example, that everyone was free to speak to whomever she chose or to read freely, but in fact they kept looking for pretexts to round on prisoners and harass them.

Feeling too weak physically to walk or sit down, I stayed stretched out most of the time. One day, a few traitresses who were passing the corner threw me looks full of contempt and said, pointing at me:

"That one wants to create an artificial climate of repression so as to say she's been under pressure."

Return to Evin

The spectacle of the "change" put on display in order to say "Excuse us, we made a mistake; don't blame Islam for that!" only lasted three months. But even during that period, the traitors sneaked in Section 4, reporting everything we did.

Once again, several Pasdaran women came into our section. They went round and chose some of us to start the "punishment spaces" exactly as before!

231

Barely three months after the cages were dismantled, the Pasdaran regrouped seventy prisoners, including me, coming from Sections 3, 4 and 7, after having spent several hours in the guards' room at Ghezel-Hessar. We were finally transferred to Evin, Section 3, which they had evacuated because of its antiquatedness. Fakour – then the director of Evin – came to make us a speech overflowing with insults and curses:

"They've picked up the filth from Ghezel-Hessar to throw it in Evin," he said, for example.

Quarter 3 was empty. When we went in, Fakour went to inspect the lavatories, but a mass of filth fell on his head. It was frankly comical and we all burst out laughing, which meant, in a way: *Did you see? You're the filth! Serve you right!*

Obviously, it was too much for that torturer who decided, to revenge himself, to take five of us away on the very first day to a particularly tough "interrogation". On returning, we were "mincemeat" as we said. There were Mehri and Soheila Rahimi, but I don't remember the names of the other three.

They confined us all, that is to say seventy prisoners, in three hermetically sealed rooms, adding, by degrees, other girls coming from Ghezel-Hessar, as well as some old inhabitants of Evin. We were very happy to be together again, as it was the first time we found each other again after so many months spent in the cages or in different sections. The torturers had, all the same, put a room at the disposal of the traitresses, from now on real mercenaries, to put us under greater pressure. The regime had "worked" on them so efficiently that they had let themselves be emptied of all humanity to become wild beasts like the Pasdaran and the torturers.

They even resembled the Pasdaran women physically: everything separated them from us. Obeying the instructions they had received, they stopped at nothing to make the prisoners suffer. They paraded through the quarter every day, throwing curses and threats at us, to intimidate us.

The gaolers opened the doors of the rooms three times a day to take us to the lavatories and the same number of times to give us food. It was a bittersweet period, although we often had to face the brutal rushing in of the mercenaries and the "hit squad" of Evin who attacked us like savage hordes, hitting, breaking and ransacking ... But bearing in mind that all that was part of our fight and our resistance against that inhuman regime, and that we were defending our humanity by doing it, nothing was unbearable any longer.

For example, there were television sets installed in the rooms. But the gaolers often came to take them away with various excuses to punish us by depriving us of a pastime and a source of information.

I remember that at that time, the regime's television was broadcasting a serial called "Sarbedaran" which told the story of a heroic resistance movement in ancient Iranian history. My friends liked that serial very much. Now the torturers didn't want us to watch it and looked for an excuse to take the set away. We were aware of their ploy. Consequently, we did all we could to avoid giving them the pretext they were looking for and above all to avoid responding to their provocations.

Every time, as soon as an instalment of the series began, they arrived vociferating:

"So they hypocrites are keeping quiet; what's happening? What are you afraid of, keeping so quiet? You like the cinema now? You've forgotten the struggle?"

In spite of these systematic provocations, they drew a blank. The new instalment began at 9 at night every Monday. We prepared for it before dinner. Once dinner was over, we put away all our things, we spread out the blankets on the ground and everyone settled down in her corner. Just before the beginning, one of the girls gave the signal: one, two, three! And we all ran to stretch out side by side and watch the TV, because there wasn't enough room for each of us to look at it while stretching out as she wished. Then we waited for the film.

At first sight, it may seem a childish game, but in the infernal conditions of the prison where the regime wanted to impose the most absolute silence and solitude, we fought against their will by coordinating our actions and gestures by concerting them collectively.

For instance, we transformed every anodyne action or gesture into a game in order to preserve that cohesion and that good temper that formed our strength in the face of the constant humiliations we suffered.

On their side, very much enervated by our behaviour, the mercenaries opened the door at 9 o'clock precisely, howling, for example:

"The hypocrites to the lavatories! Go! Get a move on!"

But nobody moved. Very angry, they swore, insulted and threatened to forbid access to the lavatories until the next morning and then slammed the door as they left. Next day, they revenged themselves, for example, by opening the lavatory doors several hours late.

The simulated executions

Every time the torturers and their apprentices started vociferating and howling, it was the signal that a new raid was on the cards that day.

One day, we heard the abominable howls of Halvaï, that bloodthirsty torturer who shouted in a very threatening voice from the bottom of No 8's basement:

"Just what do those hypocrites want? Those who've anything to say, let them come and see me!"

Then he started knocking violently on our section door before coming in. He went round all the rooms, repeating the same insanities, but nobody paid him any attention. When he saw that nobody was answering, Halvaï shouted:

Very good! You've nothing to say? But we've things to say to you!"

And he gave orders for everyone to come out of the rooms. We were in midwinter. Evin Prison is situated at the foot of the great mountain to the North of Tehran, at Shemiran, where it's always colder than in the centre of the capital. We had no shoes, so we put on light sandals, of which some had torn straps, which made walking even more difficult.

We had no idea where we were being

taken, with our eyes blindfolded. After a few minutes' walk, I had the impression that we found ourselves somewhere near the wall behind Section 209. We reached the slope of a hill that we climbed in arctic cold until the shelf at the top. The ground all around was frozen and we trembled with cold. At the top of the hill, they separated us, ordering us to stay at a certain distance from one another, without saying a word about their intentions. In spite of the blindfold over my eyes, I was able to glimpse that we were one or two metres apart. I could also see the boots of two men passing in front of us from time to time so as to watch over us in silence. I looked more attentively around my feet and I noticed a large number of cartridge cases of Kalashnikovs and Colts.

I was curious to know where we were and why we had been taken there. Taking advantage of a moment's inattention on the part of the guards, I quickly picked up a few cases, hiding them in my closed hand. I had discovered the mystery of that hill. It was the sadly celebrated hill of Evin where the prisoners were shot in groups of one or two hundred during "the execution nights" and those cases were the inanimate witnesses of those massacres.

Looking more closely, with some difficulty, I was able to glimpse traces of blood on the frozen ground and on the snow. At that moment, my thoughts flew towards my friends who had disappeared: Attiyeh Moharrer-Khansari, Tahereh Moharrer-Khansari, Fatemeh Assef, Zahra Nazari, Elaheh Oroudji, pregnant at the moment of her martyrdom, Farah Torabi, Zahra Shab-Zendedar, Homa Radmanesh, A'zam Tagh-Darreh, Fatemeh and Zahra Samimi-Motlaq, Hélène Arfa'I, Razieh Ale-Taher and Ghodsi Mohammadi, Shour-anguiz Tabatabaï, Mahdokht Mohammadizadeh, and so many others …

The faces of our martyrs kept coming to my mind. I remembered Simine Hojabr, a woman of exceptional courage. And Siba Sharifpour who had refused to reveal her name to her interrogators until the last moment. Siba, a graduate of the university and a primary schoolmistress, had been one of my best friends. Her face had been completely ravaged because of the atrocious tortures she had undergone. One day in September 1982 in Evin Prison, one of my friends with whom I had formerly worked came to see me:

"Azam, I saw someone who looked like Siba," she murmured.

Hearing the name of one of my best friends, I shuddered.

"Where did you see her?"

"I was taken to identify her during my interrogation," she answered.

We had worked together, Siba and I, during the two and a half years of political (PMOI) activities before 20 June 1981, I had learned, in the middle of the same year, 1981, that she had been arrested, by I hadn't managed to find any trace of her in prison. I thought she had been executed.

The same day at about 2 o'clock in the afternoon, the loudspeakers announced the names of several prisoners who were to present themselves for interrogation. I didn't understand why they had taken that friend to identify Siba, when they should have called me. The loudspeakers announced the names one after another and I counted them. After the nineteenth name, a little pause and then: Azam Hadj-Heydar!

I started and ran without much thought. I was led towards the row of prisoners in Section 209. A great anguish was drowning me. I asked myself where she could have been during all this time and why they had chosen that moment to call the other prisoners to identify her. I was plunged in these reflections when a man took me by my chador and murmured in my ear:

"Before you go, I'm telling you that you must keep quiet in there! You'll shut up! You'll do what I tell you to!"

While my heart was beating madly, I arrived in front of a cell. The same interrogator made me go in before shutting the inner door. He took off my blindfold, shouting:

"Don't forget what I said! One false step and you'll find yourself lying beside your dear pal! She's the one who gave your name! You see how ridiculous it is that she should be your symbol of resistance?! Look what happens to you all, at the end of that road! Save your life!"

The torturers always used those old formulas to break the prisoners down by depicting a world of absurdities where everything was useless, empty of meaning ... Although I was prepared to see Siba, I didn't recognise her at first. Her face was so damaged that she was totally unrecognisable, except ... except her smile, which convinced me that it really was she.

The interrogator was pressuring me to give her name. He started to insult me and beat me savagely, but I was categorical:

"I don't know her."

Hearing the interrogator's desperate howls and seeing his hysterical gestures, I realised that Siba had refused even to give them her name. Later on, I learned that they wanted to obtain some information before executing her and that was why they were absolutely determined to identify her.

Fixing my eyes on hers and lips and in order to be sure, I took one or two steps towards her, but the torturer hit me violently on the head with a cable, howling:

"Why did you move? I told you to stay where you are!"

"But didn't you ask me to see who it was? So I went nearer so as to see better!"

I wanted to see if she was making me a sign. Suddenly, I felt her hand move and touch my trousers but, being too weak to take hold of it, she gave up. I stayed there, flabbergasted, for a few moments before saying, with a lump in my throat:

"I don't know her. Take me away!"

But he insisted:

"You'll be sorry you said you didn't know her! It was she who said you were together …"

He went on … the same formulas, the same threats …

Faced with my silence, at last they took me back to the cell.

Over a month later, I learned that two new prisoners had been transferred to our quarter. I was in Room 1, above Section 240. I went to see them and asked their names:

"Zahra Samimi-Motlaq and Fatemeh Samimi-Motlaq."

"I should really have preferred not to see you here again, but I'm still glad to see you in our section," I said to them.

Fatemeh had a lump in her throat. She turned to Zahra:

"I think it's her."

"Who's 'she'?" I asked in a surprised and anxious tone.

All of a sudden, the thought had come to me that perhaps they were agents of the regime.

"Tell us your name so that we can give you some information," they insisted.

"Azam."

"Azam what?"

"Hadj Heydari."

It took those two sisters several minutes to overcome that state of extreme sadness and for the tears to stop flowing down their faces.

"Well, listen carefully, we're going to give you the message that was entrusted to us, before it's too late," sighed Zahra.

Their tale was so sorrowful that very often

one of them burst into tears, obliging the other to continue, and so it went on. It was in that atmosphere tinged with pain and sorrow that they told the story of the martyrdom of my dear Siba who had kept silent in front of her torturers to the end, not a word, not even her name. She had just repeated that she was a member of the People's Mojahedin. They told me that the criminal Doctor Sheikhol-Eslamzadeh often went to see her in the Evin dispensary to encourage her to betray, begging her:

"Go on, have some pity for yourself; you're still young! Just one televised confession will be enough! They really don't need that interview on TV and they won't broadcast it. It's just a way of saving your life!"

But with her triumphal smile and her heroic gestures, she had left them sadly unsatisfied. With her last words, she asked Zahra and Fatemeh to give me that message if one day they met me in the prison:

"Siba didn't even give her name. Ask all our friends who succeed in getting out of prison to give my greetings to Massoud [Radjavi] and tell him that I've done everything to stay faithful to my promise."

At that moment, on Evin hill, I don't know why I remembered all our martyrs, one by one. I was no longer trembling with cold; it was as if I felt the warmth of the martyrs' bodies in that momentary flight of my thoughts. I told myself incessantly that they had kept their promise towards God and their people. Their memory filled me with an indescribable ecstasy, so strong that, in spite of the icy wind, with no warm clothes, with a pair of torn light sandals, I stood up full of the joy of being able to rejoin them at last and also stay faithful to my oath, to my promise, to break the spell of oppression and pierce the wall of repression built by Khomeini.

For how long did I stay plunged in those thoughts? I don't know. The only thing that counted was the feeling of finding once again, at last, my friends who had fallen as martyrs. I saw myself saying to them: *You saw how I too kept my promise too? You saw that the torturer wasn't able to make me bend?*

Suddenly, one of the torturers who were

keeping guard around us gave me a terrible punch on the head. Unable to control myself, I fell on the slope of the hill. I nearly rolled down to the bottom, but he caught me by the foot and dragged me towards him, ordering me to get up and stand where I was before I fell.

"Don't you worry!" he howled, "you'll soon know the same fate as the other hypocrites! The day we decide to send you to Hell, we'll put you here, beside the others!"

A few hours later, when a large number of us had fallen to the ground after fainting because of cold, hunger and exhaustion, they took us back to 209 instead of the section where we were usually placed. They threw each of us into a cell. I had no news of the others, but I understood by contacting my friends in the two neighbouring cells in Morse, that we were alone in our cells. Our feet were frozen. Going into the cell, I rushed to the radiator in the hope of warming myself a little, but it wasn't working. I was dozing when someone put a plate of food in a corner of the cell before disappearing. The cold had weakened me so much that, in spite of my great hunger, I didn't have the strength to rise and go to the door to take the plate. At that moment, I thought they would have done better to execute me. Then I should have been freed of all those pressures, and I should have rejoined my friends whom I loved so much. But immediately I reproached myself for having given up. That was exactly what the torturer wanted. I remembered the cage episode and Hadji Davoud threatening us without stopping:

"I'll make you suffer so that you will pray to die as soon as possible ..."

So that was the torturers' aim. I imagined Hadji Davoud howling in one of his repulsive bursts of laughter:

"And yet I told you that I was a much more powerful hero than all of you! I'm the one who's brought you to your knees."

But then, I saw myself shouting at him: *You're seriously wrong, you assassin! You've forgotten the cage period too soon; you've forgotten who was brought to his knees! This time too, we'll see ...*

My body had only just grown a little warmer when someone knocked on the door: "Interrogation! Go on! Out!"

I prepared myself because I knew there would be no interrogation and they wanted to re-edit the previous evening's "show". And I was right. Although I was very tired and almost entirely exhausted, I felt morally stronger than the night before. From now on, whether they really shot us, or whether it was another simulacrum as a means of psychological torture, the scene had become an act of resistance.

The episode of the simulated executions lasted a week, during which they took us every day to the top of Evin hill to leave us there waiting, standing up, in icy cold, from the beginning of the afternoon to midnight or until dawn.

During all those hours, they threatened us, insulted us and beat us incessantly, then took us back to our isolation cells.

At the end of a week, they took us back to the old section, saying:

"All those who have a request can make it."

They thought they had punished and terrified us so much that they believed they had achieved their aim. But what an absurd idea! The prisoners regained their habits and acts of resistance. The torturers and the traitors who served them bit their fingers as they watched them.

Every day, they looked for new pretexts to round on the prisoners. For example, needles and scissors were forbidden in the section, but we had some in our cells. The women guards noticed it, noting, for example, that one or two prisoners had cut their hair; or when they saw parts of freshly sewn clothes. But in spite of their frantic searching and seeking, they found nothing and that made them mad with rage because they couldn't understand where and how we had been able to hide those tools in a practically empty room. Then they had recourse to prompt attacks in the quarter.

The only weapon for us, the prisoners, remained our collectivity. At no price did we wish to lose it. For we knew – we had paid for it with our flesh and blood – that the only means of avoiding annihilation by the torturers or turning into human waste in their hands was just to remain "together", not to lose the sense of the "collective". So we performed all tasks together, we led our incarcerated life together. In opposition to us, the torturers wanted to break that "togetherness" at any price. But, even in isolation cells, we didn't drown in thoughts centred on our personal state. We spent whole days and nights thinking of all we had done together. Lajevardi never stopped seeking means of shattering the solidarity of the Mojahedin into fragments. That was why, every day, he invented a new formula in his perverse mind: the last judgment section, cages, the residential quarters, the dormitory, the cowshed or kennel cells and many others. But he hadn't succeeded in breaking any Mojahedin prisoner with all those particularly atrocious methods. Obviously, he had broken their bodies, but not their souls fed with convictions.

In the general section

At the beginning of the year 1984, three months after our transfer to Evin, the mercenaries seemed exhausted and demoralised by the infernal conditions that they themselves had created.

Besides, they had realised that it had been a mistake to assemble the prisoners in the same place.

We were able to hear that conclusion from the mouths of Fakour and Halvaï[2].

They then decided to disperse us. One day, they divided us into groups of ten or fifteen and led us into different sectors. I formed part of a group of ten prisoners transferred to Sector 2 on the upper floor.

Before our departure, the gorilla Halvaï came to shout his usual threats at us:

"In this new sector, you must conform scrupulously to the rules! The one who disobeys had better look out!"

We entered the new sector chatting and laughing among ourselves, but we soon noticed the heavy silence that reigned there, and the sadness of the rigid faces of the prisoners who were already to be found there. We contemplated those calm faces and found

---

2. Two particularly cruel torturers.

it hard to understand the reasons for that silence. Nobody was walking in the corridors. The prisoners didn't speak to one another, not a smile, not a laugh. That collective silence pushed us into remaining silent too. We were led to our cells in little groups. After having left our things in the cell, we walked around the sector. I went to watch the television set, which was on. It was the broadcast by Mullah Ghera'ati, "the TV clown". Disgusted by his nonsense, I went towards the cell and passed M. whom I already knew. She came up to me and murmured:

"You know, Azam. It's the rule here. When Ghera'ati speaks, everyone must be quiet and listen to him."

I burst out laughing and the other new arrivals did too. Surprised, noticing that everyone was looking in our direction, she panicked and went quickly back to sit down in her place. At meal time, we noticed that each prisoner sat down, alone, in one exact place, to eat. Ignoring that state of affairs, I sat down opposite a friend and started to eat with her. One of the traitors in charge of supervision addressed herself to me:

"Go to your own place!"

"Are there names written down for each place?"

"No, it's me who decides on everyone's place!"

I ignored her and went on eating. The other new ones did likewise. Thus, in practice, we smashed a rule imposed by the torturers.

"What's happening here?" I asked one of the girls. Why are you all silent and stiff as statues?"

She told me how the traitors had made conditions intolerable, to the extent of calling the hit squads every day on any pretext, so as to beat the prisoners to death. They were conducting psychological warfare at all times by fomenting quarrels on the pretext of rules being violated, which had created this climate.

But we found those explanations unconvincing, because we had managed to make these policies fail elsewhere. Then, we discussed it and concluded that it was certainly our duty to change this graveyard atmosphere. But how to set about it? First of all, we must break the silence. The thaw made itself felt little by little. The former arrivals stated to come up to the new ones and speak to them. Among themselves, too, they had started to laugh and talk again. But it still was not enough.

One day, coming back from an interrogation, Narguesse showed me some little pebbles that she had hidden in her hand and said to me, putting them down on the ground:

"Azam, come and play 'Yeghel-Doghol[3]'!"

"'Yeghel-Doghol'? In a political prison?!"

Leila Arafa'I stated to laugh, calling out: "She's right! Let's go back to our childhood! Let's play at being those kids who will be real Mojahedin when they grow up!"

I consented to sit down on the ground and we started playing. There were only five of us at first: Leila, Mehri Hadji-Nejad[4], Mahboubeh and Narguesse, but five others joined us and we formed two teams of

---

3. A game with knuckle-bones.

4. Mehri was later able to join Ashraf Camp.

five. Within a few minutes the quarter was flooded with cries of joy and with applause as if in a real match. Two traitresses, in a fury, threw us looks filled with hatred but didn't dare intervene. Noticing that they no longer had a place in that assembly, they directed themselves towards me and, threatening me in the manner of the mullahs in filthy language that the interrogators had taught them, one of them scolded me:

"Look out, hypocrite! You're the leader who's dragged the others into this row!"

The other one threw a few insults in the direction of Narguesse who didn't hear her, she was so absorbed in the game. Finally they left the room without having succeeded in intimidating me. I remember Hengameh shouting:

"You can't do anything more; not a thing you haven't done already! So do whatever you want!"

I murmured her words.

Gradually, we organised other collective games. We preferred games whether there was an ever-increasing number of players to as to make the maximum amount of noise. We often played in teams, even for crosswords, and that added to our joy in being together. The "yoghurt" game in which several players tried to swallow whole bowls of yoghurt was one of the funniest games which the traitresses found particularly irritating. The winners received a prize, often in the shape of a portion of the best part of the next meal as well as their own share.

All means were good to make a noise and create a happy atmosphere, in order to break the graveyard calm that reigned in the section. One day, I found a slug in my plate, and put it on one side. When everyone had finished eating, I rose and said with a serious air:

"Attention, girls! Attention!"

And when they were quiet, I called out:

"I'm very sorry to have to tell you, since you've just finished eating, but you must know that this slug accompanied your dishes today. And that's why you found them particularly delicious!"

And I passed the slug to my neighbour who in her turn transmitted it to her neighbour, and so on. Everyone made comments, laughing. The traitresses, mad with rage, couldn't do anything but go on insulting and threatening us.

One day, when it was the turn for the girls in our sector to take care of preparing and distributing the meals, they discovered sticking-plasters in one of the cooking pots. We made the distribution in the various rooms, making a date at 1.30 p.m. to announce the "discovery". Everything went according to plan and at 1.30 an enormous uproar flooded the section. Thus we managed to change the climate completely, making Section 2 abandon its deathly silence. But of course, there's a price to pay for "violating the rules": sneaks' reports, followed by lashes from the interrogators or collective punishments such as locking the cell doors for several days. Nonetheless, we had all consented to pay that price in order to go on living and keep our vivacity in the face of the torturers who wanted to bury us alive. We learned a lesson, too, we new ones in Section 2 who had refused to let ourselves be impressed by the climate reigning there: a small number of people can change things if they're prepared to pay the price.

This change of atmosphere had brought the girls closer together, creating very strong bonds of friendship. Let me tell you an anecdote which may seem risible to you. I was 22 when I was arrested and was respected for that reason by the other prisoners, mostly adolescents of 15, 16 or 17. I particularly remember Mahboubeh, a schoolgirl of barely 16, a girl who was full of life, mischievous and very beautiful, who couldn't stay in one place for a minute. She was always calling me:

"Da'I! (Uncle)"

"But why do you call me that?"

"Because your kindness and sweetness remind me of my uncle!"

Narguesse, another schoolgirl, called me "Khaleh" (Auntie). It irritated the torturers and traitresses enormously. Several times, during interrogations, they threatened me:

"You hypocrite! What do you effing do in the quarter to make everyone call you 'uncle' or 'auntie'?"

The torturers used absolutely any means to inflict suffering or to terrify the prisoners. I heard prisoners in Section 209 say that they they put Massoumeh Azdanlou[5] in solitary confinement at the end of each interrogation and torture session. She was often so weak and so much at the end of her strength that she couldn't even call her guard.

One day when she was in her cell after having been atrociously tortured, the gaolers opened the door in order to throw in a snake. The reptile came slowly towards Massoumeh and stopped just beside her; it stayed there without moving. Massoumeh tracked it down, noting that it had a green skin and that it must be a river snake, therefore harmless. She then started stroking the snake, while looking calmly and gently at it. The torturers were expecting screams of fear and calls for help. But not a sound was coming from the cell. Tired of waiting, they opened the door on the pretext of bringing her food and the snake came tranquilly out of the cell, leaving the torturers dazed.

---

5. The sister of Maryam Rajavi, the leader of the Iranian Resistance.

Another common means of terrifying and torturing the prisoners consisted in putting the feet of the very young prisoners or women arrested for minor offences, during interrogations, into bags full of cockroaches or throwing rats into the cells … I remember that the first time I arrived in Section 7 of Ghezel-Hessar Prison, I saw mice and rats walking everywhere. During dinner, the procession of mice all around had frightened me at first. But once I had settled down on the third-storey bed to rest for a bit, I saw mice turning into tightrope walkers on the washing line. I watched them for a few minutes and then asked, laughing:

"Is the circus just today or is it every day?"

My neighbour, who understood that I was talking about the mice, answered smiling:

"You've only been here for two hours and you want to know everything at once? Go for a walk round the quarter and you'll understand everything."

Each to her own! The mice are playing and as for me, I'm asleep. I slept for an hour and then, feeling a mouse stroking my foot, I woke up:

"What do you do about those mice processing over your heads all the time?" I asked some girls who were arguing.

They looked at one another, laughing:

"There are lots of things like that here. You'll get used to it little by little."

One day during the pause for taking the air, I saw that Hengameh was looking at her hand, saying things, while several of our friends surrounded her, laughing out loud. I went up to her:

"Who are you talking to?"

She loosened her hand, showing me a little mouse:

"To Miss Mouse!"

Suddenly, I felt all my feelings of fear or disgust at the mice and rats fly away. We had finally learned to adjust ourselves to snakes and mice!

A fine day

One day, Alizadeh, the Pasdaran guard, rushed into the section with several traitors and howled:

"No need to go on studying French, you band of hypocrites! You'll have to learn to work at Arabic! Your boss has gone to Iraq!"

That is how we learned that Massoud Rajavi, the leader of the Resistance, had left for Iraq. Enormous cries of joy flooded the section. No doubt we hadn't understood all the political meaning of this gesture at once, but we were glad to have news of the leader of the Resistance and to know that he was safe and sound. Apart from the political explanations of this affair, the agitation of the torturers and traitresses assured us that this event was in the interest of the Resistance.

Moreover, they had been stupid enough to cut out Massoud Rajavi's photo in the newspapers and stick it on the wall; perhaps to show us that it was true. The girls went to look at that photo several times, kissed one another and burst into tears. The mercenaries who were going round the quarter to measure and report on the impact of this information were mad with rage. They circulated among us and threw out spiteful remarks so as to provoke quarrels and then call for help from Halvaï, the torturer, and his "hit squad", in short, to make our friends regret those moments of joy. But everyone ignored them.

On our side, we tried to make this information circulate in other rooms and on the floor above, while fearing to see the torturers stop everything and, worst of all, to take away the photo because of our joy. But because that line had been imposed on them by the hierarchy, the mercenaries couldn't modify it on their own initiative. Deprived of all means of information, newspapers or visits from those close to us, we considered those occasional changes of behaviour as a godsend. In the course of those six months, I will never forget the day when several of our friends fell ill. The others drummed on the door so that the Pasdaran should take them to the infirmary. The guard Alizadeh, who nourished a ferocious hatred towards the prisoners, pushed her head through the door and tracked down those who were knocking hard. She left, then came back with another guard so as to take them into their room. But the girls, who had all joined in those calls for help, prevented them.

After a few agitated minutes, Alizadeh went out howling with rage. We knew that we must expect a merciless response. It lasted barely fifteen or twenty minutes. The door was flung brutally open and that criminal Halvaï tore in at the head of his "hit squad", about twenty brutes and traitors. They were all bawling and bellowing, each one louder than the next. Knocking on the door, the bars and the walls with their coshes and whips to cause maximum terror, they opened the doors of all three rooms and started hitting the defenceless prisoners with cables and coshes, fists and feet, spewing out the most obscene insults. We ran left and right to dodge the blows, but in every corner, one of those wild beasts was ready to put us through it. We were like footballs in their hands and under their feet. They were beating us so savagely that several of us lost consciousness and crumpled up.

After an hour of unimaginable barbarity, they rounded on our modest personal belongings, stored in little bags. They threw them to the ground, scattered them, broke them, tore them. They crushed our food supplies under their boots. It's clear that they aimed to make us regret our act of resistance.

Then they pushed us into the yard with blows from their sticks and put us in a circle. They then set up a bench in the middle so as to whip the three prisoners they hated most: Soulmaz Azizi, Azam Taghdarreh and Raziyeh Ayatollahzadeh-Shirazi – all three were later executed. Once again solidarity manifested itself in a spectacular way. We were nearly a hundred and fifty prisoners and we all turned to the wall, refusing to look at their "show". Faced with this unexpected gesture, the torturers remained flabbergasted at first, before coming to themselves and struck us with another avalanche of blows.

This scene of horror lasted over two hours, until nightfall. All our heads and faces were bloodied, our limbs black with bruises. They brought us back into the cells in the same way and locked us in, thus depriving us our daily "pauses" in which to take the air.

Then, they took aim at our few books, mostly religious, such as the Qur'an, or reference books such as dictionaries, organising an auto-da-fé in the section yard, burning them with kerosene. They who so pretentiously quoted God and religion didn't hesitate to burn "God's word". Nevertheless, in spite of their sick relentlessness, they were unable to lay their hands on the books that we had carefully hidden all over the place, that we especially adored and treasured, and that were already in the prison before the fateful day of 20 June 1981.

After the attack, in spite of our wounds and our bruised bodies, we were in high spirits and felt great joy, as if we had gained a great victory. We managed to stop those criminals setting up and making a system of the inhuman method of torture mixed with humiliation, which consists in making some prisoners endure being lashed in front of the others, especially while odiously accusing them of "moral" crimes.

These moments of victory were so delicious that they freed us from the feelings of pain and humiliation aroused by torture and physical suffering. The ordeals and rough handling are as fleeting as foam on water. As soon as the Pasdaran went out, we started to talk, laugh and tell one another what they had done to each of us and what had happened. That rich and lively spirit was totally alien to the mental universe of Khomeini and his cops. Thus, every little gesture of resistance became a dagger plunged into the heart of their retrograde beliefs. That's why they were constantly making our friends undergo interrogations on our "organisation" and our activities, always asking the same questions while they hit their victims:

"Who's your boss? Who feeds you that way of behaving and sends you to your doom and your ruin?"

We found it hard to hide our joy at seeing them so desperate and we silently answered: *it's you who's being sent to your ruin and plunged into misery.*

Even today, I have a feeling of pride at having spent those years in the company of those friends and I feel pain at their absence.

But after all, perhaps they are not as absent as all that. They are certainly present in the bosoms of my sisters in the present Resistance.

Learning in prison

After that particularly violent episode, we occupied ourselves in bringing things "back to normal". We immediately agreed on a division of labour: some tidied our things, picked up the pieces and crumbs, sewed and repaired what was reparable and others took on the job of replacing, where possible, the destroyed books in order to ensure continuity in our lessons. We had programmed the free times in our day to avoid wasting time. The girls who had studied taught the subjects they had learned to groups of two or three, as larger groups would quickly have been tracked down by the spies and sneaks. And the pupils transmitted what they had learned to the others. That's how we organised courses in Arabic, English and French thanks to the girls who knew those languages very well. And others gave courses in their respective subjects. Houriyeh Beshti-Tabar, who had gained a master's degree in economic sciences, gave courses in economics. The texts consisted in little booklets put together for the occasion or newspapers that we obtained very discreetly in the waiting rooms of the interrogation rooms. Our exchanges with the other rooms or cells on various subjects also formed sources for our courses. Newspaper articles that we managed to pick up were also of use.

The second "trial"

In April or May 1986, I underwent a fresh series of interrogations and punishments because of that they called "the organisation of activities in prison". This "organisation" was nothing more than our collective life and the rejection of the regime and its torturers who wanted to deprive the prisoners of the necessary minima for remaining human beings. We resisted the pressures together.

The presidency of this court was, as in the previous trial, filled by Mullah Mohammadi-Guilani whom we called "the dinosaur" because he was lacking in the slightest human feeling. That is why he felt bestial hatred and bitterness towards anyone inspired by the ideals of the Mojahedin, any resistant, in short anyone in whom he detected traces of humanity. At the time of that "trial", I was placed opposite Guilani and two Pasdaran. One of them must be my own interrogator. But as I always had my eyes blindfolded during the interrogations, and that he remained silent during the "hearing" expressly so that I would not recognise his voice, I can't say precisely if ihe was really my usual interrogator. There were also three traitors in the guise of "witnesses".

First Guilani asked me to identify myself before shouting at me:

"Defend yourself!"

"I have nothing to say in my defence!" I answered, knowing that they had organised a scenario with those three mercenaries so as to hit me with something "strong".

Throughout those four months that I spent in "punitive detention", one of those mercenaries, Manijeh, was always rounding on me because she knew me before I was in prison.

I was right because as soon as I answered Guilani that I had nothing to say and that our ideas of logic and speech were completely opposed, Manijeh started to insult me, hitting me on the head twice over before throwing herself into a tirade of so-called "revelations" on my past in the movement before my arrest and the activities in prison, taking in the cage episode and my resistance ...

She let herself go in attacking me and spat out curses like an old witch for forty-five minutes. She was pitiable because she thought the torturers would appreciate her relentlessness and free her at once!

Then, it was another traitress, Mansoureh, who made "revelations" about me! Her method was different; less relentless and bitter, she never stop whimpering or sobbing while she told her stories, notably about the two months I had spent in quarantine. At the end of her declarations, to weaken and destabilise Manijeh even more, I called out:

"I don't know this woman and I don't know what she's talking about!"

Then the old witch started howling, shouting some more rubbish.

After her came Homa, the third traitress. She took her oath as a "witness" and, apparently in order to leave no doubt of her knowledge of me, she turned towards me:

"You know me, eh?"

She seemed quite certain that I'd answer "yes", but I firmly answered "no" and she started howling in her turn. She described our activities before imprisonment, the time spent together in Section 240, and the seven and a half months of her loyal services to the torturers, and the cage period when she "accompanied" me with all the hatred and bitterness she felt towards me. In short, it was a strange exposition, stuffed with lies mixed with a few genuine facts to "refresh my memory". I remained silent. Not a word. The sentence fell: definitely five years of prison and ten suspended.

Thus the "trial" ended.

I no longer remember if they made me sign something after the sentence was read out. But on leaving the "court", they kept me standing up for a few hours and each one of the torturers or the mercenaries who passed in front of me threw me a few words on the fate awaiting me in order to frighten me more. The three traitresses who themselves admitted they had dreamed of a very heavy sentence of me were the most relentless.

But after having seen the Hell of the cages and the prison in general, nothing mattered to me any more. My victorious silence irritated them. I knew they were trying to provoke me so as to take advantage of my reaction:

"What's happening?"

"Insolent Azam's keeping quiet!"

"She's grown shy!"

Freed!

After the second "trial", they summoned me two or three more times to the interrogation room. They wanted me to participate in an interview, but I categorically refused. At once exasperated and hysterical, the interrogator kept hitting me with his whip and threatening me:

"I shan't let you fulfil your dream of

being a heroine! I'll keep you here until you're completely

rotten!"

And he kept repeating Hadji Davoud's classic refrain:

"I'll keep you here until the day when you hair becomes as white as your teeth and your teeth become as black as your hair is today!"

One day, in September 1986, they summoned me again. In the middle of the usual flood of insults, they let fall:

"We know you're a 'hypocrite' and if you get out of here, you'll rejoin your organisation. But we'll set you free so as to catch you again and cut you in pieces."

I had lost all hope of liberation for some time, but that day I quickly understood that they were going to set me free. Then in my thoughts I undertook at once that if I was liberated I would do exactly what they dreaded most. That is to say that I should work above all to regain contact with my organisation and rejoin it.

A week later, on 14 September, they summoned me to the interrogation room.

They wished to stop me picking up messages from my friends in prison so as to transmit them outside after my liberation.

Obviously, I didn't believe in my liberation until the last moment. I thought at first that it was a fresh interrogation following a fresh report from the spies. I entered the office in the room, feeling suspicious. And the Pasdaran wanted to preserve that suffocating atmosphere until the last minute: they started to murmur, pointing at me.

However, they finally, through the loudspeakers, called my friends to get my personal belongings ready, which they quickly did before giving them to the guards. I was amazed, flabbergasted. Was I really going to be separated from my dear friends with whom I had lived through those sad or joyous moments? This separation was incredibly painful to me. At once, I remembered our strikes, our protests, the punishments, the torturers' violence and our acts of resistance. I was leaving all that and my friends were staying on the other side of the wall! Suddenly, I couldn't hold back my tears. The Pasdaran, criminally stupid, thought I was afraid of being moved. They mocked me, sniggering and pointing. I felt that pain especially when one of them shouted, laughing:

"But you're free, you imbecile!"

I thought of that painful separation. How would I leave without them in a society dominated by Khomeinists? What was I to do and how should I live and breathe in a society like that? I thought of all these things and those imbeciles sniggered, unable to imagine for an instant what was going through my head!

That was when I took my decision: I must go.

Especially as, a few months earlier, I had laughingly asked Farah, one of the girls on the point of being freed, to leave a trail outside if she decided to leave one day, so that I could rejoin her if one day I was freed. I had added:

"Because my family are Khomeinists and I've nobody to help me rejoin my organisation."

At that crucial moment, I thought of

that exchange with Farah: was it possible that she had left a trail? Otherwise, where would I find a means of making contact? After five and a half years of captivity, I had no idea of the state of society.

I was plunged in those confused thoughts when the Pasdaran, after having searched my things, gave me back my bag and led me back, with blindfolded eyes, to the interrogation office. They repeated the same threat to my elder sister, Mahine, who had come to find me in front of the prison:

"If she tries to rejoin the PMOI, this time she'll be flayed alive!"

Mahine was seized with panic. A few months later when our younger sister Najmeh and I called her to tell her that we were abroad, she nearly fainted with joy because she had been terribly afraid all the time that we'd be arrested again.

To tell the truth, I was no less anguished than she was at the thought of being behind the bars again. Because I had seen or heard a great deal about what they did to the girls who had tried to rejoin the organisation after their liberation. But I told myself: *Have you ever thought you would be freed one day? Didn't you tell yourself that perhaps there would be no return every time you were taken to be interrogated? So, what's changed? The regime is still in place. It's killed most of the people you cherished; some of them are still within its claws, in its throat. What security and what life under this regime? Under that infernal power, people die every day. Every time I catch sight of Pasdaran, every time the telephone rings unexpectedly, every time I go to the prosecutor's office for the weekly signature, I die and come back to life; whereas if I get myself killed while crossing the frontier, I'll die once for all!*

That's how, my sister Najmeh and I, both of us very determined, decided to rejoin our other brothers and sisters in the heart of the Resistance on the other side of the frontier, in Iraq.

An extraordinary and dangerous adventure was about to begin, but while crossing the mountains of Kurdistan on foot, I thought only of getting out of Iran, imprisoned in the claws of the mullahs. We had to proceed without hesitation, without yielding, in order to go on being human. I missed those with whom I had lived and fought in the hardest moments: Tahereh who, first of all, had shown me the way, my dear Siba, my brave Shouri, my little Mahboubeh, and all the others who overturned my life for ever my showing me that the humanity in everyone knows no limits.

I had to find my own people again, all those men and women who had rejoined the resistance. A difficult road full of anguish, that had to be crossed on foot, although we were crushed by weariness and tormented by hunger.

We finally knew relief when, after crossing the frontier, I saw the first Mojahedin call out a warm "Welcome!" to me and to Najmeh. Pressing her in my arms was like finding all my vanished friends again.

Years have passed and my fight continues in Ashraf, that city of resistance near the Iranian frontier. Ashraf is a town built by the Mojahedin in a desert 70 km from the frontier with Iran and about a hundred kilometres North-east of Baghdad. For about twenty years the Mojahedin have been living there and fighting the mullahs' regime. We are three thousand four hundred survivors of the prisons and massacres, some of us having lost all our families in the repression, but all determined to rid Iran of the mullahs' grasp. A blockade, restrictions imposed by the Iraqi authorities linked to Tehran, the lack of medicaments, of fuel and of the most necessary items will not make us yield. In July 2009, the Iraqi forces supported by the regime's agents launched an attack on the defenceless, unarmed inhabitants of Ashraf. Eleven of us were killed, and five hundred wounded. But we resisted once again, as we confronted Halvaï's savage horde in Evin. The regime's agents, using the same methods as in the prisons, send us traitors, agents in the service of the Ministry of Information, to threaten us, insult us and keep up intense psychological pressure at the entrance to the city. But whatever they do, Ashraf embodies the resistance of the 120,000 political prisoners who accepted neither humiliation nor dishonour. They continue to inspire the Iranian people in their quest for freedom.

APPENDIX

Portraits of women in the resistance executed under the mullahs' regime

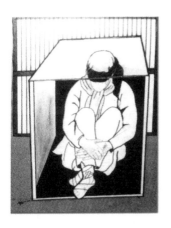

Ashraf Rajavi

Massoumeh Azdanlou

Fatemeh Ayatollah-Zadeh
Shiraz (Razieh)

Nahid Izadkhah-Kermani

Atieh Moharer-Khansari

Tahereh Moharer-Khansari

**Farideh Torabi
(Farah Bayat)**

Fatemeh Samimi-Motlagh

Fatemeh Mahmoud-Hakimi

Hélène Arfa'i

Ellaheh Orouji

Massoumeh Karimian
(Shouri)

Sima Hakim Maani

Simine Hojabr

Roghieh Akbari

Siba Sharifpour

Table of Contents

THIRD PART

Captivity

FOURTH PART

Two worlds confront each other

Table of Contents

FIFTH PART

The result of the war

APPENDIX